best
hikes
with
dogs
COLORADO

Ania Savage

THE MOUNTAINEERS BOOKS

Dedication

This book is dedicated to the Colorado Mountain Club members and their invariably well-trained and well-behaved dogs. The club's "doggie hikes" are a joy—great opportunities to learn and to make new friends, both human and canine.

THE MOUNTAINEERS BOOKS
is the nonprofit publishing arm of The Mountaineers Club, an organization founded in 1906 and dedicated to the exploration, preservation, and enjoyment of outdoor and wilderness areas.

1001 SW Klickitat Way, Suite 201, Seattle, WA 98134

© 2005 by Ania Savage

All rights reserved

First edition, 2005

No part of this book may be reproduced in any form, or by any electronic, mechanical, or other means, without permission in writing from the publisher.

Published simultaneously in Great Britain by Cordee, 3a DeMontfort Street, Leicester, England, LE1 7HD

Manufactured in the United States of America

Acquiring Editor: Cassandra Conyers
Project Editor: Laura Drury
Copy Editor: Julie Van Pelt
Cover and Book Design: The Mountaineers Books
Layout: Mayumi Thompson
Cartographer: Moore Creative Designs and Judy Petry
All photographs are by the author unless otherwise noted.

Cover photograph: Photo by Jim Martin
Frontispiece: *Looking toward the Elk Range*

Maps shown in this book were produced using National Geographic's *TOPO!* software. For more information, go to *www.nationalgeographic.com/topo*.

Library of Congress Cataloging-in-Publication Data
Savage, Ania.
  Best hikes with dogs. Colorado / by Ania Savage.— 1st ed.
    p. cm.
Includes bibliographical references.
  ISBN 0-89886-968-4
  1. Hiking with dogs—Colorado—Guidebooks. 2. Colorado—Guidebooks. I. Title.
SF427.455.S38 2004
917.88—dc22
                                    2005001121

CONTENTS

Part 1: Hiking with Your Dog

Part 2: The Trails

Fort Collins

Nederland/Eldora

Boulder/Lyons

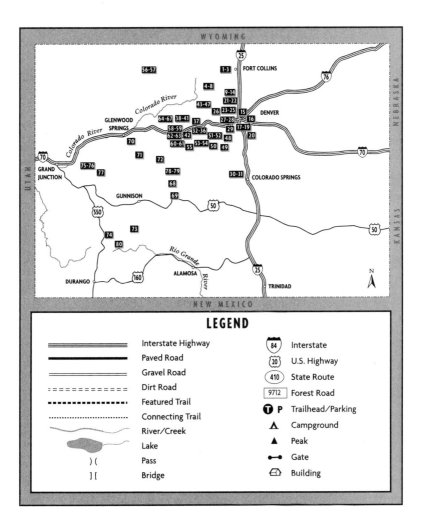

LEGEND

Interstate Highway	
Paved Road	
Gravel Road	
Dirt Road	
Featured Trail	
Connecting Trail	
River/Creek	
Lake	
) (Pass	
] [Bridge	

84 Interstate	
20 U.S. Highway	
410 State Route	
9712 Forest Road	
T P Trailhead/Parking	
▲ Campground	
▲ Peak	
•—• Gate	
⌂ Building	

HIKE SUMMARY TABLE

Hike	Easy on paws	Easy hike	Possible backpack	High altitude	Alongside stream most of hike	Lake to swim in	Some or all no leash	Solitude	For athletic dogs	For senior dogs	Forest for entire hike	Alpine scenery
1 Browns and Timberline Lakes	●		●	●		●			●	●		●
2 Blue Lake (Rawah Wilderness)	●		●	●	●	●			●	●	●	
3 Dunraven Trail/North Fork of Big Thompson River	●	●			●				●	●	●	●
4 Lake Isabelle and Pawnee Pass	●	●	●			●	●			●	●	●
5 Mitchell and Blue Lakes	●	●	●			●	●			●	●	●
6 Arapahoe Pass and Lake Dorothy	●		●	●			●	●	●	●		●
7 Woodland Lake, Lost Lake, and Skyscraper Reservoir	●	●	●	●	●	●	●		●		●	●
8 King Lake and Devils Thumb Loop	●		●	●	●	●			●	●		●
9 Ceran St. Vrain Trail and Miller Rock	●	●			●		●		●			●
10 Royal Arch	●								●		●	●
11 Green Mountain Loop	●	●							●		●	●
12 South Boulder Peak and Bear Mountain	●		●						●		●	●
13 Mesa Trail South End	●	●								●		●
14 Flatirons Vista and Doudy Draw	●	●			●					●		●
15 Platte River Greenway: Adams County	●	●			●					●		
16 Sand Creek Greenway	●	●						●		●		
17 High Line Canal: Blackmer Lake	●	●			●					●		●
18 High Line Canal: Horseshoe Preserve	●	●			●					●		●
19 Cherry Creek State Park	●	●			●		●			●		
20 Castlewood Canyon State Park					●				●			●
21 Windy Peak	●	●				●				●	●	●
22 Frazer Meadow	●	●			●					●	●	●
23 Beaver Brook Trail and Braille Nature Trail					●				●		●	
24 Apex Trail/Enchanted Forest					●				●		●	
25 Bear Creek Trail through Four Parks	●								●		●	

Hike	Easy on paws	Easy hike	Possible backpack	High altitude	Alongside stream most of hike	Lake to swim in	Some or all no leash	Solitude	For athletic dogs	For senior dogs	Forest for entire hike	Alpine scenery
26 Elk Meadow off-leash area and Bergen Peak	●	●					●		●		●	●
27 Plymouth Mountain	●	●		●					●		●	●
28 Meadowlark Trail Loop	●	●			●						●	
29 High Line Canal: Waterton Canyon	●	●			●		●		●			
30 Waldo Canyon Loop	●	●							●			
31 The Crags	●	●		●						●	●	●
32 Silver Dollar and Murray Lakes	●	●	●		●	●				●		●
33 Mount Wilcox and Otter Mountain	●		●		●	●	●	●				●
34 Rosalie Trail	●		●	●	●			●	●		●	●
35 Square Top Lakes	●		●		●	●	●	●				●
36 Square Top Mountain	●	●	●		●	●		●				●
37 Grizzly Gulch	●	●		●		●	●		●	●	●	●
38 Herman Lake	●		●	●	●			●				●
39 Pettingell Peak	●		●		●	●	●	●				●
40 Watrous Gulch	●		●		●	●	●			●	●	●
41 Woods Mountain and Mt. Machebeuf	●		●		●	●	●			●		●
42 Mount Sniktau			●		●	●	●			●		●
43 Mount Flora	●	●	●	●		●	●	●				●
44 Colorado Mines Peak and Blue Lake	●	●	●		●	●	●			●		●
45 Stanley Mountain	●	●	●			●	●	●				●
46 West Fork of Clear Creek	●		●			●	●	●				●
47 Butler Gulch	●	●	●		●		●	●		●	●	●
48 Goose Creek	●		●	●					●	●		
49 Brookside-McCurdy Trail			●	●				●	●	●		
50 Ben Tyler Trail	●		●		●	●	●			●	●	
51 Scott Gomer Trail and Abyss Lake Trail	●		●	●	●		●	●			●	●
52 Three Mile Creek Trail	●	●	●	●			●	●			●	●
53 Kenosha Pass East	●	●	●		●		●	●	●		●	●

Hike	Easy on paws	Easy hike	Possible backpack	High altitude	Alongside stream most of hike	Lake to swim in	Some or all no leash	Solitude	For athletic dogs	For senior dogs	Forest for entire hike	Alpine scenery
54 Kenosha Pass West	•	•						•		•	•	•
55 Georgia Pass	•		•					•	•	•	•	•
56 Service Creek Trail	•		•		•			•	•		•	
57 Fishhook Lake, Lost Lake, and Lake Elmo	•	•			•	•			•	•	•	
58 Straight Creek	•	•		•	•		•			•		•
59 Chihuahua Gulch and Lake	•		•		•	•	•	•	•			
60 McCullough Gulch	•	•			•	•	•			•	•	•
61 Crystal Lakes	•			•	•	•	•	•	•			•
62 Meadow Creek Trail	•		•	•				•	•		•	•
63 Searle Pass	•		•				•	•	•			•
64 Wheeler Lakes	•		•			•		•	•		•	
65 Uneva Pass	•		•	•				•	•			•
66 Pitkin Lake	•		•	•	•	•		•	•		•	•
67 Booth Falls and Booth Lake	•		•		•	•			•		•	•
68 Kroenke Lake	•		•	•	•	•	•	•	•		•	•
69 Waterdog Lakes	•	•	•	•	•	•	•			•	•	•
70 Lost Man Trail Loop			•	•	•			•	•			•
71 Maroon Lake, Crater Lake, and Buckskin Pass	•		•	•		•			•			•
72 Hardscrabble and Williams Lakes	•		•		•	•	•	•			•	•
73 Waterdog Lake	•	•				•	•	•	•		•	
74 American Basin	•	•				•	•	•	•			•
75 Water Dog Reservoir to Twin Basin Reservoir	•	•				•				•		
76 Mesa Lakes and Lost Lake	•	•				•				•		
77 Crag Crest National Recreation Trail Loop						•			•			•
78 Mount Belford and Mount Oxford	•		•	•			•		•			•
79 Mount Antero	•		•	•			•		•			•
80 Handies Peak	•		•	•			•		•			•

AUTHOR'S NOTE

I was afraid of dogs as a child and young adult and still remember with deep regret passing up the opportunity to adopt a lost German shepherd because of my fear. Then when my children were in grade school, their begging and whining made me finally cave in and our family got a golden retriever, the gentlest and most lovable of dogs. And thus my love affair with dogs began and has continued to this day.

I think animals can sense your attitude toward them and if you are nervous or afraid, that feeling will be transmitted to them and may lead to problems or unexpected confrontations.

Over the years I have made friends with and have had for longer or shorter periods of time, two border collies and a Labrador-rottweiler mix. My extended family has also had dachshunds and miniature poodles. I must admit that my affection still lies with golden retrievers.

In my experience, bigger and stronger dogs do better on trails in the backcountry than smaller and less-athletic dogs. The same is true of people. Long-legged hikers seem to cover the ground effortlessly, while those of us who are shorter, smaller, or less wiry tend to have a harder time keeping up.

That said, hiking with a dog no matter the breed is fun simply from the sheer delight your dog takes in being out on the trail. The "doggie hikes" of the Colorado Mountain Club are those that I remember most vividly, generally with a grin.

Dogs on a hike display their personalities. A border collie tends to shepherd the entire procession of dogs and owners, dashing from the front to the back and to the front again, making sure that everyone is still where human or dog should be.

Younger and less-experienced dogs need to be trained for the trail and not be confronted with an environment that is unfamiliar and perhaps even frightening to them. I remember a young German shepherd on his first doggie hike scaling a big boulder. He thought he could just jump up on it, lost his footing, slid, and lay spread-eagled, howling and frozen with fear.

As caretakers of our pets, we should not ask the impossible of them. A dog that is old should not be asked to scale a Fourteener. He will try and may end up with bleeding paws and heatstroke. When I talk to U.S. Forest

Hiking partner (Photo by Stefan Krusze)

Service rangers in Colorado and ask about dogs on trails and in the high country, I often hear horror stories of lost dogs or frantic phone calls asking for rescue of an injured or stranded dog. Since the use of the backcountry is at an all-time high, and we want to take our pets along for the exercise and the joy of the trek, incidents involving dogs are becoming commonplace.

Yes, we love the company of our dogs. They make a hike so much more interesting. Their keen sense of smell and their acute vision will often direct our gaze to a critter we may have otherwise not seen. They warn us about lurking dangers. The enthusiasm that a dog shows on a hike is also infectious. It makes the hardest switchback bearable, especially since our dog will stop and look back at us panting uphill to make sure we are okay.

Yet, the responsibility of making the hike safe and enjoyable rests with us solely and completely. For that reason, when selecting hikes for this book, I made a conscious effort to offer a variety of hiking adventures for every type of dog in every physical condition, from an overweight couch potato to a muscular retriever.

So take your dog hiking, after carefully researching the hike and making certain that both of you are up to the rigors of the trek. Hiking is hard work, sometimes a dangerous undertaking. But a hike is also what you make it. Look forward to a hike with the same eager anticipation that your dog will exhibit once he knows both of you are on your way. Dogs are the best trail companions. They offer companionship without a litany of complaints and they won't break into inconsequential chatter when you want solitude.

ACKNOWLEDGMENTS

Dog lovers know the places dogs love most and many have shared with me their favorite hikes during casual encounters on many trails in Colorado. Special thanks are due to Barb Evert, Amy Lange, and Marilynn Clark, Colorado Mountain Club hike leaders and dog lovers. Many Forest Service rangers in the Arapaho, Roosevelt, Routt, White River, and Grand Mesa National Forests offered advice on trail selection, corrected misconceptions, and exhibited extraordinary patience when answering numerous questions. The rangers at the Dillon Ranger Station of the White River National Forest were particularly helpful.

I am also indebted to Terrence "TJ" Rapoport, executive director of the Colorado Fourteeners Initiative, for providing the organization's guidelines on dogs hiking Fourteeners; to Kate Kramer, executive director of Sand Creek Regional Greenway Partnership, Inc., for the latest maps of the

CMC doggie hike, Chihuahua Gulch

greenway; to Marc Pedrucci of the Adams County Department of Parks and Community Resources, for details about the extension of the Platte River Greenway to Brighton; to Mitchell Martin, one of the park managers at Castlewood State Park, for walking the trail to ascertain the length of various segments and for a GPS map of the trail; and to Ben Lawhon, education director of Leave No Trace Center for Outdoor Ethics.

Finally, this book has been enhanced by the photographs taken by Jim Gehres, Stefan Krusze, and Yue Savage, who together with Charlie Savage hiked to double-check trails when I could not do so.

PART 1

Hiking with Your Dog

*D*ogs are wonderful hiking companions and their delight in the sights and smells of a new trail is contagious. As long as they are well behaved, healthy, and friendly, you could not ask for a more congenial trail companion than a dog. Dogs throw themselves wholeheartedly into the adventure of the hike.

However, the quality of the experience for your dog will often be in direct proportion to the care and preparation you provided prior to the trip. This means that you have an obligation not only to investigate if your dog will be welcome in the areas you plan to explore, but also to go prepared for a variety of situations that both you and your pet may encounter. Hiking Colorado's Rockies, especially at altitude, can quickly become a calamity for both pet and owner if the hike is too difficult or if you go into the backcountry unprepared. To help you plan, here are some tips for making your outdoor outings with your dog as safe and enjoyable as possible.

Getting in Shape and Training

Getting in shape for hiking is building stamina and endurance. This is what athletes do. This plan will also work for your dog. Start with daily walks of a mile or so, building up the distance gradually to around 5 miles round trip. If you plan to have your dog pack in his own gear, this is the time to teach Rover to carry a pack. You can start the process at home by placing a small towel across his shoulders. If he shrugs it off, persist and eventually Rover will learn to tolerate it. When he is ready to graduate to a pack, measure him around the rib cage to determine the pack size. A dog pack should fit securely without hindering the dog's ability to walk and run. It should hug the shoulders as closely as possible without limiting movement. The straps that hold the dog pack in place should be placed where they will not cause chafing. The pack typically has panniers or cargo pouches on either side. Start training your dog with an empty pack. Next, add small bottles of water or some crumpled paper to create bulk. The rule of thumb is that the load should *never* exceed one-third of your dog's body weight.

Nutrition is another consideration in training your dog. A complete and balanced diet will boost your dog's energy during a hike. But moderate the amount of food before a hike. Feed your dog after the hike and make sure he is rested before attempting another one.

Consistent training and good nutrition is also the prescription for you getting in shape for hiking. When training on short, easy hikes in the plains or on more challenging ones in the foothills, wear your boots and the pack you will carry in the mountains.

Next, graduate to elevation. Experiment with short hikes at altitude and evaluate how both of you do. Remember, air is thinner at altitude and your lungs have to work twice as hard. The same is true for your dog.

Your dog has two advantages over you that may actually get him into trouble—training and practice can help you avoid mishaps. First, dogs are generally much more agile on rocks and steep terrain than we humans are. However, a dog that is not trained to deal with boulders or sheer drop-offs may become paralyzed with fear even if you are nearby. Forest Service rangers in Colorado recount innumerable stories of hikers seeking help not for themselves but for their stranded dog.

The second advantage your dog has—and one you should exploit—is your dog's keen sense of smell and sight. So, if your dog suddenly stops, pricks his ears, and points in a certain direction, follow his gaze and you may see a critter that you would have otherwise missed. But also make sure that your dog does not go off chasing wildlife. This is particularly important on tundra, where ptarmigans, marmots, and picas make their home—animals not used to seeing or dealing with dogs.

Some dogs like to carry their own walking stick on a hike. (Photo by Stefan Krusze)

On every hike, you are the leader and the caregiver your dog looks to for direction. Be a good leader by building trust, friendship, and respect. If you make training and exercising a pleasant experience, your dog will listen to you and you will be ready for any challenge.

The Ten Essentials for Humans

For many, hiking is a method for challenging physical limits and for expanding tolerance of the exacting and unknown. Yet, to go unprepared—with no maps or compass, not enough water, or without warm clothing and rain gear—is foolhardy and puts both you and your canine companion at risk.

On the other hand, a hiker properly equipped will more than likely have a successful outing. Essential equipment includes broken-in hiking boots over wool socks on your feet and an extra pair or two of socks (wool and nylon) in your pack; quick-drying pants, not jeans; a lightweight, wool or synthetic-fiber shirt, not cotton; a hooded jacket or parka; a warm hat; rain gear; and plenty of water, plus at least one meal.

Here is a list of ten essentials adopted by mountain clubs across the country:

Ten Essentials: A Systems Approach

1. Navigation (map and compass)
2. Sun protection (sunglasses and sunscreen)
3. Insulation (extra clothing)
4. Illumination (headlamp or flashlight)
5. First-aid supplies
6. Fire (firestarter and matches/lighter)
7. Repair kit and tools (including knife)
8. Nutrition (extra food)
9. Hydration (extra water)
10. Emergency shelter

—The Mountaineers

In addition, it is also imperative that you tell a friend or a family member where you and your dog are going, and sign in at the trailhead if a register is available.

The Ten Essentials for Canines

Dogs need to be outfitted, too. Here is a list of canine essentials you cannot leave home without:

Max Von Schattenjager, a sable German shepherd (Photo by Stefan Krusze)

1. Obedience training. Before you set foot on a trail, make sure your dog is trained and can be trusted to behave when faced with other hikers, other dogs, wildlife, and an assortment of strange scents and sights in the backcountry.
2. Doggie backpack. Lets the dog carry his own gear.
3. Basic first-aid kit (see Canine First-Aid Kit)

4. Dog food and trail treats. Bring more food than your dog normally consumes since he will be burning more calories than normal, and if you do end up having to spend an extra night out there, you need to keep the pup fed too. Trail treats serve the same purpose for the dog as they do for you—to generate quick energy and a pick-me-up during a strenuous day of hiking.

5. Water and water bowl. Don't count on there being water along the trail for the dog. Pack enough extra water to meet all your dog's drinking needs.

6. Leash and collar, or harness. Even if your dog is absolutely trained to voice command and stays at heel without a leash, sometimes leashes are required by law or just by common courtesy, so you should have one handy at all times.

7. Insect repellent. Be aware that some animals, and some people, have strong negative reactions to DEET-based repellents. So, before leaving home, dab a little DEET-based repellent on a patch of your dog's fur to see if he reacts to it. Look for signs of drowsiness, lethargy, and/or nausea. Restrict bug repellent applications to those places your dog can't lick—the back of the neck and around the ears (staying well clear of the ears and inner ears) are the most logical places mosquitoes will be looking for exposed skin to bite.

8. ID tags and picture identification. Your dog should always wear ID tags, and I heartily recommend microchipping your pooch as well. To do this, a veterinarian injects a tiny encoded microchip under the skin between your dog's shoulders. If your dog ever gets lost and is picked up by animal control, or is taken to a vet's office, a quick pass over your dog's back with a scanner will reveal the chip and speed Rover's return to you. Microchipping is so prevalent that virtually every vet and animal shelter automatically scans every unknown dog they come in contact with to check for chips. The picture identification should go in your pack. If your dog gets lost, you can use the picture to make flyers and handbills to post in the surrounding communities.

9. Dog booties. Use these to protect your dog's feet from rough ground or harsh vegetation. They are also great at keeping bandages secure, should your dog damage his pads and need some first aid.

10. Compact roll of plastic bags and trowel. You'll need the bags to clean up after your dog on popular trails. When conditions warrant, you can use the trowel to take care of your dog's waste. Just pretend you are a cat—dig a small hole several inches deep in the forest duff, deposit the dog waste, and fill in the hole.

I also like to wrap a colorful bandanna around my dog's neck. This can help you spot your pet among trees and, during hunting season, a piece of cloth will distinguish your dog from game.

Trail Etiquette

Out on the trail you are the ambassador for all hikers and their dogs. Some people you meet may believe that your dog does not belong in the backcountry. Others may be afraid of your dog. You need to be friendly and Rover must be on his very best behavior in such situations. On the bright side, a canine companion may serve as an icebreaker as other hikers stop and ask about your pet.

Permits and Regulations

Remember that most of the public lands in Colorado require that a dog be on a leash. Dogs are not permitted in Rocky Mountain National Park and in some state parks, such as Roxborough State Park, just south of Denver. Dogs must also be on a leash in metro Denver Open Space, in Jefferson County Open Space, in Denver Mountain Parks, and in all wilderness areas. Along the Front Range, Boulder County permits hiking with your dog off-leash and under voice command. National forests and Bureau of Land Management areas permit off-leash dogs, but even these agencies impose the leash rule on some heavily used trails.

The American Dog Owners Association, in concern for the health and safety of dogs in the backcountry, has developed a list of reasons why dogs should be leashed when in the backcountry:

- Leashes protect dogs from becoming lost and from run-ins with wildlife such as mountain goats, marmots, ptarmigans, bears, and sick, injured, or rabid animals.
- Unleashed dogs intimidate other hikers and their leashed dogs, depriving them of the peace wilderness provides.
- Unleashed dogs harass, injure, and sometimes kill wildlife.
- A leashed dog's keen senses can enhance your awareness of nearby wildlife or other wilderness visitors.

Riley taking a snow bath

- Unleashed dogs increase the probability of dogs being banned from your favorite public lands.
- Failure to leash your dog may result in a fine.

Note the last item in the list. Forest rangers take a very dim view of dogs chasing wildlife and the fines escalate dramatically after the first offense.

But rules should not prevent you from having a grand time with your dog. A dog that walks sedately at your side or is ahead of you exploring new scents should have been trained to be well behaved long before you both set foot on the trail.

Weather Safety

On any high-altitude hike in the Colorado Rockies, be prepared for sudden weather changes, snow drifts in the middle of the summer, and sometimes people who should not be there in flip-flops and without water. Mountain rescue is a staple news story in Colorado, both in winter and summer. Of course this does not mean that you should stay home after all the training, conditioning, and gear packing. Simply, before leaving, know the risks and know how you are going to deal with them if one or more arise.

First, don't dawdle at home. Get up and leave early. Starting early makes it possible for you to get a good parking spot at the trailhead and to reach your hike destination by noon, so that you can be on the way down if an afternoon lightning storm rolls in suddenly.

Second, whatever the time of day, be aware of the sky and cloud cover. Many of the hikes in this book take you and your pet above timberline for many hours at a stretch. Ridge walking offers fabulous vistas and solitude but little shelter from a sudden lightning storm.

In Colorado, thunderstorms are practically a daily phenomenon in late spring and summer. Tall puffy cumulus clouds turn purple quickly and fast-moving lightning storms are common in the afternoon. Plan your hikes so that you and your dog will be hiking back to timberline by early afternoon.

If you see lightning or hear thunder, retreat to below timberline. If you are caught on the tundra during a storm, keep a good grip on your dog while discarding any metal frame backpacks or dog collars. Stay low to the ground and never stand under a lone tree or present the tallest point around. Retreating to timberline should always be your strategy.

Every summer a few mishaps occur because hikers do not use common sense to turn back when purple thunderstorms form. Seasoned hikers advise, "The mountain will be there the next time you come."

Finally, beware of hypothermia, an always-present threat when hiking the Colorado Rockies. Layer your clothing and keep in mind that the temperature at the trailhead might have been 70 degrees with no wind, but above timberline, it might only be 45 with a biting wind, gusting to 30 or 40 miles per hour. Always pack some extra wind and rain gear even if the weather forecast predicts no rain for the entire week.

Keeping Your Dog Healthy

When hiking on the high plains or in the foothills or on mesas, make sure to check your pet's paws for burrs and his coat for ticks that can cause Rocky Mountain spotted fever.

If your dog is panting excessively or drinking water excessively, he might be overheating. Dogs sweat through their noses and paws and they don't cool as efficiently as humans do. So you need to keep your dog properly hydrated and make sure he does not get overheated, a condition that can lead to heatstroke or heart palpitations. Hydration is especially important on a hot day and above timberline.

Dogs, like humans, are susceptible to water parasites, including *Giardia*. Hikers and campers should filter, boil, or chemically purify water obtained from streams. However, for dogs, *Giardia* hazard is impossible to guard against. Unless a water source is obviously tainted, the advice is to not worry about it. Telling a thirsty dog that he can't lap water and wallow is almost impossible to explain or enforce. You can bring water with you to limit your dog's drinking from streams and lakes.

Debbie and Russell take a water break. (Photo by Yue Savage)

Wildlife Hazards

There are black bears and mountain lions in Colorado. Forest rangers advise not taking your dog into an area where such animals live. If you do camp out with your dog, make your camp bear-safe (keep your camp pristine and hang all food), and make certain that your dog does not wander away from camp.

Other animals, such as raccoons, porcupines, and beavers, can also hurt a dog. Dogs have been gored by mountain goats, which are common in the Colorado Rockies. Prevention is the best solution. Keeping your dog in sight and under control at all times will go a long way toward preventing nasty bites and dangerous confrontations.

On the high plains and in the foothills, rattlesnakes are more of a threat to dogs than to humans. Dogs that wander off the trail into the brush are vulnerable. If your dog is bitten, abort the hike and seek veterinary assistance. Here again, keeping a dog on a leash and under control can avert a disastrous confrontation.

First Aid

Even when you are most prepared, the unforeseen happens when you least expect it. For that reason you should carry a small first-aid kit for yourself and one for your dog. The most common hiking injuries suffered by dogs are footpad cuts and scrapes. If your dog begins to limp or looks uncomfortable, check his paws. If need be, clean any cut and put on a dog bootie over the injured paw. If your pet gets a cut or scrape, proper first-aid care should be administered immediately.

Canine First-Aid Kit

Having a dog first-aid kit is essential, even if it has the bare-bones essentials. Something is better than nothing. For a complete, comprehensive canine first-aid kit, though, anyone heading into the wild with a canine companion should carry the following essentials for the dog's first aid:

Instruments:
- Scissors/bandage scissors
- Toenail clippers
- Rectal thermometer (note: healthy dog should show a temperature of 101 when taken rectally)

Cleansers and disinfectants:
- 3% hydrogen peroxide
- Betadine
- Canine eyewash (available at any large pet supply store)

Topical antibiotics and ointments (non-prescription):
- Calamine lotion
- Triple antibiotic ointment (Bacitracin, Neomycin, or Polymyxin)
- Baking soda (for bee stings)
- Vaseline
- Stop bleeding powder

Medications:
- Enteric-coated aspirin or Bufferin
- Imodium A-D
- Pepto-Bismol

Dressings and bandages:
- Gauze pads (4 inches square)
- Gauze roll
- Non-stick pads
- Adhesive tape (1-inch and 2-inch rolls)

Riley gets a boot.

Miscellaneous:
- Muzzle
- Dog booties
- Any prescription medication your dog needs

For extended trips, consult your vet about any other prescription medications that may be needed in emergency situations, including:
- Oral antibiotics
- Eye medications
- Ear medications
- Emetics (to induce vomiting)
- Pain medications and anti-inflammatories
- Suturing materials for large open wounds

Leave No Trace

To minimize environmental impact, you and your dog should remain on the trail, especially in those areas where trail modifications have been made to reduce human impact. Hiking on weekdays also minimizes human impact, offers solitude, and diminishes trail and campground

Opposite: Aspen stroll at Kenosha Pass

congestion. The increasing use of the backcountry necessitates that hikers, especially those accompanied by dogs, take personal responsibility to preserve and protect the wilderness. The Colorado Fourteeners Initiative and the Colorado Mountain Club, as well as other hiking and environmental organizations, urge every hiker to adopt minimum-impact hiking and backpacking principles. The principles derive from the outdoor ethics maxim: "Leave no trace!"

Guidelines for Minimum Impact

- Carry out all trash, even gum wrappers.
- Use existing trails and do not cut across switchbacks.
- Protect vegetation from damage, especially on the tundra at high altitude.
- Use a camp stove and avoid building campfires.
- Avoid using soaps in streams. Dispose of soapy water in buckets at least 50 feet from streams.
- Camp at least 200 feet from a stream.
- Dispose of human and dog waste by covering it with 6 to 8 inches of topsoil at least 200 feet from all open water and trails.
- Keep dogs on leash or where permitted, under voice control.
- Leave what you find, especially old buildings, and do not pick wildflowers.

Dogs on Fourteeners

If you have never hiked a Colorado Fourteener, beware the description "easy."

Fourteeners—the fifty-four peaks in Colorado that are 14,000 feet or higher—are never easy simply because they are very high mountains. You and your dog are hiking where the air is thin and your lungs—and your dog's—have to work twice as hard.

True, some Fourteeners are easier to scale than others, but any such mountain is an undertaking and should not be taken lightly. Even the easiest Fourteener has talus and scree slopes toward the top and the trail over boulders can be slippery and dangerous. Ascending a Fourteener takes more preparation and thought than hiking in the foothills. You need to take a number of precautions to ensure a safe climb to and from the summit for yourself and your dog.

Being physically fit is key. Knowing that your dog has trail-hardened paws is equally important. If you are not sure on either point, hike a lesser

Goats near Chihuahua Lake

mountain, such as Mount Sniktau (Hike 42), that replicates the altitude and the rocky terrain of a Fourteener without most of the uphill climb. You might also consider taking your dog by car to high altitude to see how he does. Mount Evans (14,264 feet) and Pikes Peak (14,110 feet) have paved roads to the summit.

Next, the timing of a Fourteener climb is crucial. Ask experienced Colorado hikers and they will say, "Reach the summit by noon." As noted in Weather Safety above, high-country weather is surprising, fast moving and dangerous. Furious thunder-and-lightning storms on Fourteeners are common, swooping in from nowhere with vicious lightning, eardrum-splitting thunder, and torrential rain, snow, or hail. If you ever have had the misfortune of getting caught in one of these storms, you will never forget it. If your dog shakes at the sound of thunder at home, he will be petrified and possibly not controllable in a storm on a Fourteener.

Getting to the top of a Fourteener by noon does not guarantee that you will escape a storm, but it helps. A well-conditioned hiker can reach the summit of many Fourteeners in about 5 to 6 hours. Therefore, start from the trailhead by 6:00 or 7:00 AM Expect a 4- to 5-hour descent.

The popularity of bagging Fourteeners is at an all-time high. This has prompted the Colorado Fourteeners Initiative (CFI) to set out the following guidelines for taking dogs up Fourteeners. I have discussed much of this above, but it bears repeating:

- Most Fourteener trails do not have a constant water supply nearby such as a lake or river. Please carry additional food and water for your dog.
- High altitude affects dogs the same as humans. Watch for signs of distress, nausea, or exhaustion in your dog and take breaks for your dog to rest.
- Keep in mind that dogs' sensitive paws are exposed to high-altitude elements such as sharp rocks and freezing snow.
- Please carry doggie bags to pick up and carry out your dog's waste.
- It can be difficult and sometimes dangerous to hold a leash while hiking if your dog is not properly leash trained.
- Dogs can sometimes become scared and confused when forced to climb rocks, boulders, or talus they are unfamiliar with.
- If climbing in a nonwilderness area, check with the county to inquire about local leash laws. Leash laws are in effect in all wilderness areas.

The CFI also asserts that the presence of dogs on Fourteeners may have devastating impacts on alpine wildlife. Domesticated dogs are several steps removed from the natural wildlife found in alpine ecosystems and dogs off-leash are prone to chase wildlife. This threatens the health of wildlife and disturbs the balance of existing predator/prey relationships. An animal that is forced to flee from an unnatural predator uses up energy reserves it is conserving for hibernation. With a short growing season and limited food supplies, this can substantially reduce the chances that the animal will survive the harsh winter of the alpine environment.

Fourteener hikers hike responsibly with their dogs when they keep them on a leash, provide a good example for other hikers, show consideration of other visitors, and respect the natural ecosystem of the fragile alpine environment.

The Fourteener hikes in this guide are Mount Bedford and Mount Oxford (Hike 78), Mount Antero (Hike 79), and Handies Peak (Hike 80). These were selected based on two criteria: First, the presence of a road partway up the mountain mitigates a dog's impact on the ecosystem. Second, the tundra terrain and the absence of huge boulders or extensive scree or talus slopes on these mountains means that a properly trained and trail-hardened dog should not encounter such problems as bleeding paws or be terror-stricken by drop-offs.

Once you and your dog reach the summit of a Fourteener, remember to sign the register to record your achievement! Summit registers for all Fourteeners and for some of the more significant Thirteeners are archived and maintained by the Colorado Mountain Club. The registers are usually in metal pipes with PVC caps, and are usually found in the rockpile cairn at the summit. Add your dog's name next to yours when you sign in.

How to Use This Book

High plains, deep canyons, rolling meadows, soaring peaks—the variety of Colorado's topography is astonishing. An hour's drive can take you from suffocating heat and prickly cacti of the desert-like flats to a cold, windswept, and snowdrift-lined pass on the Continental Divide. This guide attempts to capture the diversity of Colorado's landscape in 80 hikes that range from easy ones on flat terrain in the Denver metro area to tough ascents up Fourteeners.

All hikes are on public land or on public access through private land, the latter near trailheads in more populated areas or where in the past there was significant mining activity or homesteading.

All but four hikes in this book stay on trail for their entire length. Although some breathtaking and dog-friendly sites are off-trail, bushwhacking presents hikers and their pets with added dangers, especially if you are in an area with a leash requirement (picture you and your pet tangled in underbrush). The three hikes in this guide that go off-trail—Mount

Field of bistort

Wilcox and Otter Mountain (Hike 33), Woods Mountain and Mount Machebeuf (Hike 41), and Colorado Mines Peak and Blue Lake (Hike 44)—are above timberline to prevent such problems. A very short bushwhack is also included in Ceran St. Vrain Trail and Miller Rock (Hike 9), and Bear Creek Trail (Hike 25), essentially eliminating extra mileage in retracing a trail loop.

Overall, hikes range from very short trails to long backcountry adventures to summit climbs and ridge walks along the Continental Divide. Day hiking predominates and offers a wide choice in trail length, difficulty, and destinations. Overnight backpacking can be quite challenging and requires more extensive planning and preparation, but there are some of those, especially along the Colorado Trail (Hikes 53, 54, 55, and 63), the Brookside-McCurdy Trail (Hike 49), the Ben Tyler Trail (Hike 50), and in the Park, Gore, and Sawatch ranges (see Hikes 56 and 57, 62, 64, 65 and 68, respectively).

Some obvious criteria were used to select the hikes. The first was the condition of the terrain. An attempt was made to select hikes with terrain suitable for dog paws. We hike in heavy boots. Our dogs don't enjoy that protection.

Fun at Herman Lake

Hikes along streams were chosen over those with little or no access to water. Hikes to lakes were also favored. Above timberline, hikes on soft tundra were chosen over hikes on gravel, scree, or talus. Boulder-hopping hikes were avoided, as were hikes that require passage on narrow or knife-edge ridges.

There are a few exceptions to these rules. Mount Sniktau (Hike 42) has no shade, little tundra, many rocks, breathtaking altitude, and a mean tailwind. Yet it was chosen because it is a relatively safe hike in adverse conditions. Do this hike before attempting to climb a Thirteener or Fourteener. The experience will tell you whether you and your pet are ready for tough, high-altitude hiking.

All hikes are for no-snow conditions, although some routes, such as the one up Butler Gulch (Hike 47), are popular winter snowshoes.

Pink elephants at Straight Creek

And, of course, there are the intangibles that make one hike memorable and another one so-so. For me, panoramic vistas that calm the soul were as important as the soft tundra for my dog's paws. The abundance of wildflowers also made me select the colorful hike over one less visually exciting. Special seasonal features, such as the molten-gold show of aspen in the fall, convinced me to select two hikes on Kenosha Pass (Hikes 53 and 54).

The organization of this book is straightforward. The hikes are grouped north to south along mountain ranges and east to west across the state, except three hikes that ascend Fourteeners, which are grouped separately because of their difficulty and the extra thought that these climbs require. In the jumble of mountain ranges in central Colorado, hikes are organized by the corridors—the access routes that climb and descend the backbone of the American continent. Winter hiking in Colorado requires additional precautions, speed, and stamina.

Each hike begins with summary information, including distance, hiking time, high point, elevation gain, the best hiking time, recommended maps, and agency contact information. After the summary information come driving directions and the hike description.

Hiking time is a subjective calculation, so you and your dog may need more or less time for a hike. Elevation gain records the cumulative uphill portions of a hike—if you hike down on your way in and up on your way out, this is counted in the total gain for the hike. Listed maps are U.S. Geological Survey (USGS) 7.5-minute series and Trails Illustrated topographic maps; sometimes park brochures are suggested. Agency phone numbers appear in each hike; full addresses are listed in Appendix A: Contact Information and Resources, where you will also find other organizations of interest to dog lovers.

The hike descriptions are guides and cannot substitute for good judgment and careful preparation. This guide makes no provision for the many variables that affect a hike, especially one that involves a climb above timberline. Time of day, weather, your physical condition and that of your dog, and the possibility that you may fail to locate the described route or landmarks, determine the success and safety of a hike.

Hopefully, this guide will provide information that will help you plan safe and enjoyable outings with your dog.

A Note About Safety

Safety is an important concern in all outdoor activities. No guidebook can alert you to every hazard or anticipate the limitations of every reader. Therefore, the descriptions of roads, trails, routes, and natural features in this book are not representations that a particular place or excursion will be safe for your party. When you follow any of the routes described in this book, you assume responsibility for your own safety. Under normal conditions, such excursions require the usual attention to traffic, road and trail conditions, weather, terrain, the capabilities of your party, and other factors. Keeping informed on current conditions and exercising common sense are the keys to a safe, enjoyable outing.

The Mountaineers Books

PART 2

The Trails

FORT COLLINS

1. Browns and Timberline Lakes

Round trip: 8 miles
Hiking time: 6 hours
High point: 11,430 feet
Elevation gain: 2100 feet
Best hiking time: July–September
Maps: USGS Kinikinik and USGS Comanche Peak; Trails Illustrated Poudre River, Cameron Pass (no. 112)
Contact: Roosevelt National Forest, Canyon Lakes Ranger District, (970) 295-6700

Getting there: From Fort Collins, travel 11 miles north on U.S. Highway 287 to the hamlet of Ted's Place. Turn left (west) onto Colorado Highway 14 and continue for 26 miles to a turnoff on your left (south) onto County Road 63E (Pingree Park Road). Continue south for 5 miles to Forest Road 139 (Crown Point Road). Turn right (west) and drive 12 miles to the Browns Lake Trail trailhead, which is at the intersection with another dirt road. Parking is on the right side of the road. Cross the road to the trailhead.

The trail starts off as an old jeep road that winds its way through a thinning limber pine forest before rising above timberline. The rest of the hike

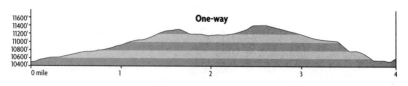

One-way

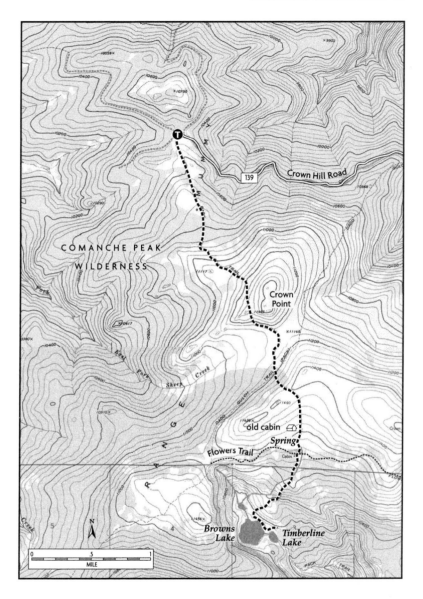

is across tundra to two lakes hidden deep in a cirque, where snow may linger into July. On this hike, the starting and ending elevations are about the same. This means that you drop down to the lake after climbing several ridges and then have to climb out of the cirque on the return. The views along the way are worth the climb. From high points along the hike

Wild and beautiful Cache la Poudre canyon

you can see the Mummy Range to the south, the Medicine Bow Range to the west, and the Snowy Range in Wyoming to the north.

A reliable spring is about three-fourths into the hike, the only water source until you reach the lakes. Be sure to bring sufficient water for yourself and your dog so that both of you are well hydrated, especially if the day is hot. This hike is in the Comanche Peak Wilderness and leash laws apply.

Sign in at the trailhead register and continue through the sparse forest and occasional stands of pine on increasingly uphill terrain to reach the first ridge at 1.7 miles. Pass the wilderness boundary. Crown Point, (11,463 feet) is the rocky knob to your left, and panoramic vistas open before you in all directions.

Descend into the valley between the two ridges for the next 0.5 mile. Reach the summit of the second ridge at 2.5 miles and begin your descent to the lakes. At 3 miles, the trail crosses the Flowers Trail that bisects the tundra east to west. You'll find the spring here. An old cabin, purportedly used by sheepherders at one time, is nearby. This is a good place to stop for a break, water, and a snack.

The trail drops sharply from here to Browns Lake, some 800 feet below. It is the larger of the two lakes and is the first one you will reach. A stream connects Browns and Timberline Lakes. After a rest and a dip for your dog in one of the lakes, begin the uphill climb back to the trailhead.

The Browns Lake Trail continues for another 1.3 miles southward. It passes to the east of Timberline Lake and descends again to intersect the Beaver Creek Trail. If you turn left (east) on the Beaver Creek Trail, you will reach Comanche Reservoir in less than 1 mile.

2. Blue Lake (Rawah Wilderness)

Round trip: 9 miles
Hiking time: 7 hours
High point: 10,800 feet
Elevation gain: 1500 feet
Best hiking time: June–October
Maps: USGS Chambers Lake; Trails Illustrated Poudre River,
   Cameron Pass (no. 112)
For more information: Roosevelt National Forest, Canyon Lakes
   Ranger District, (970) 295-6700.

Getting there: From Fort Collins, travel 11 miles north on U.S. Highway 287 to the hamlet of Ted's Place. Turn left (west) onto Colorado Highway 14 and drive through the beautiful Cache la Poudre River canyon for 53 miles to Chambers Lake. The trailhead is on the right (north) side of the road, about 1 mile past the Chambers Lake turnoff. There is a blue trailhead sign.

Lone hiker at the start of the trail (Photo by Yue Savage)

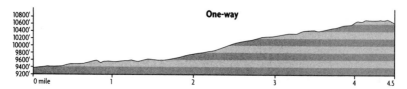

The road to this trail runs through the rugged and beautiful canyon created by the Cache la Poudre River, which, like the Big Thompson River (Hike 3), originates in the steep peaks of Rocky Mountain National Park. The drive is a scenic delight as the canyon walls rise on either side of the road. Chambers Lake is located at the mouth of Poudre Canyon and the Blue Lake trailhead is just past the lake. Tall spruces and firs shade the trail for most of the hike, and it is a pleasant trek even on a hot day, with a constant source of cooling water for your dog.

Since the Blue Lake Trail enters the Rawah Wilderness, wilderness leash laws apply. Camping is not permitted within 0.25 mile of Blue Lake.

The trail is well signed with blue-diamond markers as it descends rapidly into the Joe Wright Creek drainage and crosses a bridge over the creek. The trail then curves northwest and begins a slow upward climb that offers occasional views of Chambers Lake to the right (east). A scant 1.5 miles from the trailhead, the trail crosses Fall Creek on a bridge and follows the creek up its drainage as it passes into the Rawah Wilderness.

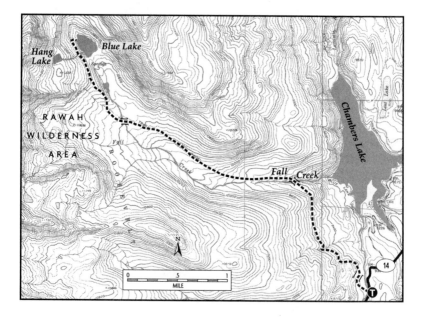

Another creek crossing comes at just over 3 miles into the hike, a little below the outlet of an unnamed small lake that lies south of Blue Lake. This area is known as "lake country" and is dotted with sapphire-colored lakes, large and small. The forest thins here and the trail passes through two meadows that are a riot of ever-changing colors during the summer months. This is a great place to stop and relax before the last steep pitch.

Next, the trail crests the ridge and offers up a vista of Blue Lake. To reach the lake, however, you need to leave the main trail and drop about 100 feet down a steep treeless slope into the sculpted cirque that holds the lake.

From the ridge itself, the panoramic view looks to the north at the Mummy Range and Rocky Mountain National Park. Hang Lake, a small lake to the left (west) of Blue Lake and a few hundred yards off the trail, beckons further exploration. Return the way you came.

3. Dunraven Trail/North Fork of Big Thompson River

Round trip: 5.5 miles
Hiking time: 6 hours
High point: 8800 feet
Elevation gain: 800 feet
Best hiking time: May–September
Maps: USGS Glen Haven; Trails Illustrated Cache la Poudre, Big Thompson (No. 101)
For more information: Roosevelt National Forest and Canyon Lakes Ranger District, (970) 295-6700

Getting there: Take Interstate 25 north from Denver to exit 34, Loveland. Drive west through Loveland and take U.S. Highway 34 west to Drake. Turn right onto County Road 43 and travel approximately 6 miles. Turn right onto Dunraven Glade Road (there is a Forest Service access sign) and drive to the end of the road. Park in the small parking lot adjacent to the trailhead and restroom.

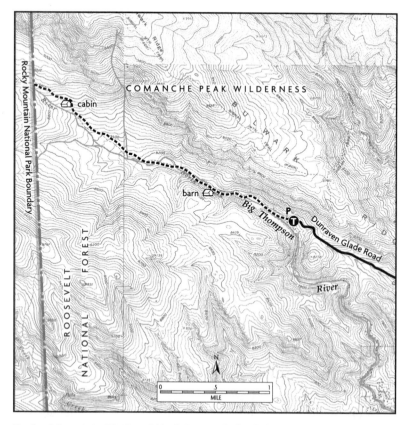

Rocky Mountain National Park is a park for hikers but not for dogs or other pets. Dogs are restricted to parking lots. However, there are numerous trails in the vicinity of the park that lie in the Roosevelt National Forest and are accessible to you and your pet. One of these is the Dunraven Trail along the North Fork of Big Thompson River. This trail begins outside the lightly used northeast corner of the park and ends at the Lake Ranger Station inside the park (even though you and your dog will stop at the park boundary). This trail crosses through the Comanche Peak Wilderness and so leash rules apply.

The Dunraven trailhead is about 3 miles from the national park boundary. The well-marked trail follows the stream and makes half a dozen stream crossings over plank or log footbridges, allowing plenty of water access for your dog. The early section of the trail goes through private land, so please stick to the trail. You will pass an old open-sided barn and a horse corral across the stream from you in this stretch.

In August and September, wild raspberries mature along the trail where the forest thins. Just before you reach the clearly marked national park boundary, you will come into a clearing with a ruined cabin. This was once part of a rustic hunting resort for the wealthy. It closed in 1914, one year before the national park was founded. There are several camping sites in the area and the stream is nearby.

A local tale claims that somewhere in this area, the Scottish Lord Dunraven buried a cache of whiskey one fall, with the intent of unearthing it the following year when he returned. The cache, however, was never found and possibly remains buried to this day. The snowcapped rounded mountain that you glimpse through the trees is Mummy Mountain, named after a Colonel Mummy, a friend and hunting companion of Lord Dunraven.

Prairie on the trail

NEDERLAND/ ELDORA

4. Lake Isabelle and Pawnee Pass

Round trip: 7 miles
Hiking time: 6 hours
High point: 12,541 feet
Elevation gain: 2050 feet
Best hiking time: June–September
Maps: USGS Ward; USGS Monarch Lake; Trails Illustrated Indian
Peaks, Gold Hill (no. 102)
For more information: Roosevelt National Forest, Boulder Ranger
District, (303) 541-2500, Sulphur Ranger District, (970) 887-4100,
Indian Peaks Wilderness Information Line, (303) 541-2519

Getting there: From Boulder, take Canyon Road west from U.S. Highway 36. This road becomes Colorado Highway 119. Drive to Nederland, where you turn right (north) on Colorado Highway 72 and drive to Ward. On the outskirts of Ward, look for a sign to Brainard Lake. Take that paved road west to the Brainard Lake ranger booth. Continue past the lake, following signs for Long Lake. The road ends at a parking lot and a road roundabout.

Lake Isabelle may well be the jewel of the Brainard Lake Recreation Area and the Indian Peaks Wilderness. There are many hikes with lovely vistas,

abundant wildflowers, and beautiful streams. Lake Isabelle scores a 10 in each category. Thus, the crowds are plentiful, but if you get an early start, go midweek, or go far enough, you will escape most other hikers.

Because of the area's popularity, the Forest Service has imposed the following use fees: $1 per pedestrian, $5 per vehicle, $5 for an overnight camping permit (June 1 through September 15). A season pass is $20. Camping fees end September 15. Entrance fees end around November 1. Dogs are allowed but must be on a leash at all times.

Find the trailhead that says Long Lake/Pawnee Pass at the west edge of the parking area. Proceed on a well-defined trail through dense forest. In 0.25 mile, Long Lake comes into view. The trail turns to a boardwalk over the swampy area alongside the lake. The boardwalk has a turnout that offers a view up and down the length of the lake.

Once past Long Lake at 1 mile, switchbacks take you to a turnoff for Lake Isabelle. Take the left trail fork down to Lake Isabelle, about 0.25 mile from the main trail and 2 miles from the trailhead. The lake is at 10,868 feet, an elevation gain of only 350 feet from the trailhead.

In this subalpine, well-watered region, wildflowers grow abundantly along the slow-moving streamlets and rivulets. Find a place among them so that you also have a view downvalley to Long Lake and beyond. Your dog will surely find a pleasant wet spot nearby.

It is hard to leave this lovely area, but to continue, return to the trail fork. A sign there points toward Pawnee Pass, 1.5 miles and a hefty 1700 feet of elevation gain ahead. A series of log bridges take you across tumbling streams that offer additional opportunities for your dog to enjoy. Steep switchbacks take you above timberline, where a large, flat meadow opens up.

At the end of the meadow, the trail narrows and rises through a talus

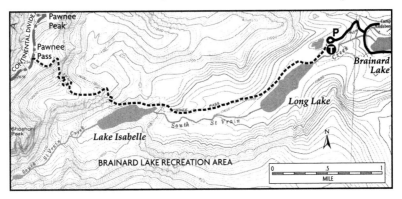

Looking east from Lake Isabelle to Long Lake

slope to a saddle, which is the summit of the pass (12,541 feet) and also the Continental Divide. To your right is Pawnee Peak (12,943 feet) and to your left is Shoshone Peak (12,967 feet). If you hike a little down the slope you will look west into the broad valley where Lake Granby lies. Beyond is the Gore Range. Return the way you came.

Backpacking: This hike also lends itself to a 2- to 3-day backpack. You can continue on the trail down from Pawnee Pass past Pawnee, Crater, and other lakes to the town of Granby and Lake Granby. If you do this backpack one-way, you need to arrange for transportation from Granby. To reach Granby, take Interstate 70 to U.S. Highway 40. Drive over Berthoud Pass past Winter Park and Fraser to Granby.

5. Mitchell and Blue Lakes

Round trip: 5.4 miles
Hiking time: 4–5 hours
High point: 11,400 feet (11,800 to tarn)
Elevation gain: 1000 feet (1400 feet)
Best hiking time: June–September
Maps: USGS Ward; Trails Illustrated Indian Peaks, Gold Hill (no. 102)
For more information: Roosevelt National Forest, Boulder Ranger District, (303) 541-2500, Indian Peaks Wilderness Information Line, (303) 541-2519

Getting there: From Boulder, take Canyon Road west from U.S. Highway 36. This road becomes Colorado Highway 119. Drive to Nederland,

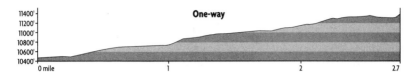

where you will turn right (north) on Colorado Highway 72, which will take you to Ward. On the outskirts of Ward look for a sign that says Brainard Lake. Take that paved road west to the Brainard Lake ranger booth. Continue past Brainard Lake, following signs for Mitchell Lake. The trail is at the end of a road roundabout.

Parts of the Brainard Lake Recreation Area overlap into the Indian Peaks Wilderness. This area offers spectacular scenery, a variety of hiking trails, more than half a dozen lakes, camping facilities, and picnic areas with tables, drinking water, and toilets. Parking is tight by noon on summer weekends. An early start is advised, or hike this popular area during the week. Although crowded, the area is very much worth the trip.

Because of the area's popularity, the Forest Service has imposed the following use fees: $1 per pedestrian, $5 per vehicle, $5 for an overnight camping permit (June 1 through September 15). A season pass is $20. Fees end around November 1. Dogs are allowed but must be on a leash at all times.

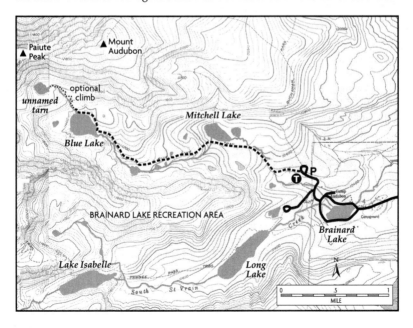

A ridge of mountains, dominated by Mount Audubon, far right, above Blue Lake

This hike starts in a forest, then proceeds along a stream, passes an alpine lake, and reaches timberline and another alpine lake rimmed by towering peaks. Along the way, there are numerous opportunities for your dog to get wet, and enjoy the streamlets, rivulets, streams, and lakeshore.

Start at the Mitchell Lake trailhead on a well-marked path through a lush forest. The trail is muddy in the spring and after a wet spell. Continue 0.8 mile to Mitchell Lake on your right. Take a rest here to admire the scenery and let your dog lap water along the shore. There are some big boulders here, but there are plenty of access points to the edge of the water. Continue hiking through thinning scrub vegetation to timberline and Blue Lake.

Standing at the end of the trail at Blue Lake, the vista of jagged peaks is breathtaking. The very large mountain to the right (north) is Mount Audubon (13,223 feet). Next to it (to the left) is Paiute Peak (13,088 feet). Straight ahead is Mount Toll (12,979 feet), named after Roger Toll of the National Park Service. To the left is Pawnee Peak (12,943 feet).

To explore more, look for a social trail to your right that follows Blue Lake's shoreline to the north. This trail leads to a high point and a vista of the valley you came up. By now, you will be alone, since most hikers turn around at Blue Lake.

If you want complete solitude for yourself and your pet, there is a tiny lake directly below the southeast face of Paiute Peak. To reach it, scramble steeply northwest to a shelf where the tarn lies. You will ascending 400 feet in 0.4 mile and the going is steep and rough. So be prepared and watch the weather.

6. Arapahoe Pass and Lake Dorothy

Round trip: 6.3 miles
Hiking time: 5 hours
High point: 12,061 feet
Elevation gain: 1950 feet
Best hiking time: July–September
Maps: USGS East Portal; USGS Monarch Lake; Trails Illustrated
    Indian Peaks, Gold Hill (no. 102)
For more information: Roosevelt National Forest, Boulder Ranger
    District, (303) 541-2500, or Sulphur Ranger District, (970) 887-4100

Getting there: From Boulder, take Canyon Road west from U.S. Highway 36. This road becomes County Road 119. Drive to Nederland and south on Colorado Highway 72. Drive 0.6 mile, then turn right (west) onto paved County Road 130 and follow signs for Eldora Ski Resort and the town of Eldora. Drive through the town of Eldora and continue west as the pavement ends. The gravel road is maintained and is passable in a passenger car. At the fork in the road, go right. Continue for 4 miles to the Buckingham Campground. The Fourth of July/Arapahoe Pass Trail trailhead is at the far end of the upper parking lot.

This moderate and beautiful hike takes you to the Continental Divide by way of the valley created by the North Fork Middle Boulder Creek drainage. The campground and trail are very popular on weekends, so it is wise to get to the trailhead early. However, most hikers turn around at the Fourth of July Mine or veer off on a trail to Diamond Lake. Permits are required for backcountry overnight stays June 1 through September 15; contact the Boulder Ranger District.

The well-marked and well-defined Arapahoe Pass Trail rises in switchbacks through a conifer forest. It then enters a meadow that is abloom with wildflowers in July. At 1.2 miles, bear right at the junction

One-way

12500'
12000'
11500'
11000'
10500'
10000'
0 mile   1   2   3 3.15

with the Diamond Lake Trail. In another mile the terrain levels off as the trail emerges into scrub vegetation below timberline. Here, at 11,245 feet, are the remains of the Fourth of July Mine that produced silver in the 1870s.

Nearby is the intersection with the Arapahoe Glacier Trail. Stay on the Arapahoe Pass Trail as it continues west on an old mining road. The trail climbs the narrowing valley to the pass, which is 1.2 miles ahead. Once at the pass (11,906 feet), follow a less distinct trail for 0.25 mile across boulder-strewn and moderately rising terrain southwest to Lake Dorothy (12,061 feet) for another 155 feet in elevation gain.

Depending on when you do this hike, the lake may still be icebound. Your pet, however, may enjoy getting his paws wet or even taking a dip in the frigid water. Boulders surround the lake and snowfields linger for a long time here. So bring along warm gear if you plan to lunch by the lake. A dog that has worked hard climbing to the pass may enjoy a cooling roll in any remaining snow. Return the way you came.

Backpacking: From the pass, the Arapahoe Pass Trail turns right (north) and drops 750 feet on steep switchbacks to Caribou Lake, a popular camping area. From Caribou Lake the trail descends to Coyote Park

North and South Arapahoe Peaks rise above trail to Arapahoe Pass.

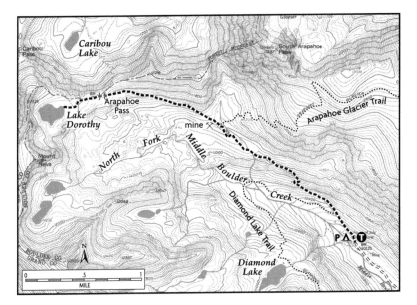

and then follows Arapahoe Creek to Monarch Lake, which can be reached from Granby.

7. Woodland Lake, Lost Lake, and Skyscraper Reservoir

Round trip: 9 miles
Hiking time: 8 hours
High point: 11,221 feet
Elevation gain: 2200 feet
Best hiking time: June–September
Maps: USGS Nederland; USGS East Portal; Trails Illustrated Indian Peaks, Gold Hill (no. 102)
For more information: Roosevelt National Forest, Boulder Ranger District, (303) 541-2500

Getting there: From the roundabout in Nederland, follow Colorado Highway 72 south for 0.6 mile, then turn right (west) on paved County Road 130. Follow signs for Eldora Ski Resort and the town of Eldora. Drive through the town of Eldora and continue west as the pavement ends. The gravel road is maintained and is passable in a passenger car.

At the fork in the road, go left. Follow signs for the Hessie townsite. You can park at the abandoned mining town or continue another 0.25 mile up a rough and often puddled jeep road to the Hessie trailhead. The parking area here is small, so if you don't want to hike that extra 0.25 mile, get to the trailhead before 10:00 AM at the latest.

You have a choice of three lovely lakes on this hike and your dog will love all three. The first lake—Lost Lake—is an easy jaunt from the trailhead. Woodland Lake is farther up the Jasper Creek drainage and over some steep climbs into a lovely valley. Skyscraper Reservoir is at the very top, up another shelf and into the cirque below the Continental Divide.

In addition to the awe-inspiring vistas for you and the opportunity for several refreshing dunks for your dog, the trail itself is a pleasure. You and your dog can hike side by side along several broad segments, and at times the ground is not only soft but downright boggy—easy on canine paws.

Some of the meadows are wet, especially in early summer, so take along mosquito spray. The Woodland Lake Trail, about 2 miles into the hike, is

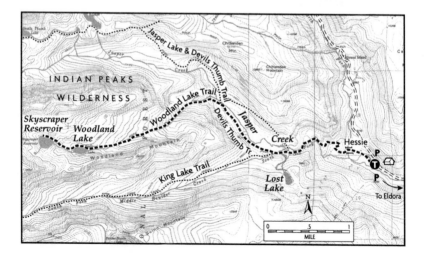

Devils Thumb is visible from Woodland Lake.

in the Indian Peaks Wilderness, so wilderness leash regulations apply. Camping is permitted near the lakes and in the meadows. Permits are required for overnight stays, June 1 through September 15; contact the Boulder Ranger District.

Start at the Devils Thumb Trail trailhead (also the way to Devils Thumb Pass on the Continental Divide; see Hike 8). Begin hiking by crossing the footbridge and taking the Devils Thumb Trail, which climbs for 0.5 mile on an old road. In 0.8 mile, just before a bridge over the South Fork Middle Boulder Creek, the Devils Thumb Bypass Trail forks right (north). Stay on the main trail as it flattens out and passes into a pleasant meadow where it again follows an old road along the creek.

At 1.2 miles intersect with the Lost Lake Trail. It veers to the left (south) and continues on an easy uphill for 0.4 mile and an elevation gain of about 150 feet to a broad shelf. At the north end of Lost Lake there is a large beaver lodge you might like to investigate. Families hiking with children often make Lost Lake their destination.

Back on the main trail, another trail junction comes in a short 0.2 mile. King Lake Trail heads left (west); stay on the main trail. Shortly after this junction, the Devils Thumb Trail enters the Indian Peaks Wilderness. It continues on fairly level terrain for another 1 mile to the Woodland Lake Trail junction. In places, Jasper Creek may have spilled over its banks and the trail is muddy. Temporary alternative trails run on either side of the wet spots; try to stay on the main trail.

Turn left (west) onto the Woodland Lake Trail and begin climbing in a southwesterly direction. For a while, the trail again follows an old road. Reach Woodland Lake in 2 miles, or just over 4 miles from the trailhead. Make sure to locate to the northwest the dramatic view of Devils Thumb, the 600-foot granite tower that dominates the skyline above Devils Thumb Lake.

The adventurous hiker, accompanied by a trail-hardened dog, may want to push on to the next and final lake on the trail. Continue along the north side of Woodland Lake and up the rocky headwall above the lake. In another 0.5 mile, the trail ends at Skyscraper Reservoir where your dog can enjoy a swim while you eat lunch.

8. King Lake and Devils Thumb Loop

Round trip: 14-mile loop
Hiking time: 13 hours or backpack
High point: 12,400 feet
Elevation gain: 3300 feet
Best hiking time: June–September
Maps: USGS Nederland; USGS East Portal; Trails Illustrated Map Indian Peaks, Gold Hill (no. 102)
For more information: Roosevelt National Forest, Boulder Ranger District, (303) 541-2500

Getting there: From the roundabout in Nederland, follow Colorado Highway 72 south for 0.6 mile, then turn right (west) on paved County Road 130. Follow signs for Eldora Ski Resort and the town of Eldora. Drive through the town of Eldora and continue west as the pavement

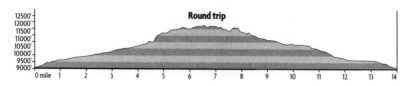

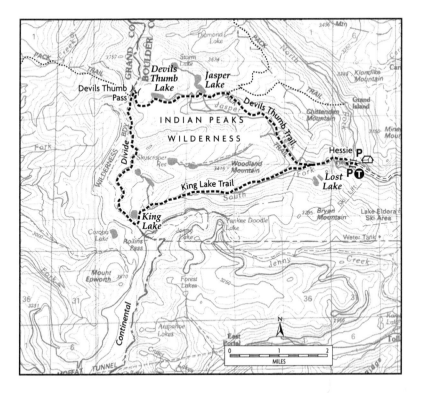

ends. The gravel road is maintained and is passable in a passenger car. At the fork in the road, go left. Follow signs for the Hessie townsite. You can park at the abandoned mining town or continue another 0.25 mile up a rough and often puddled jeep road to the Hessie townsite. The parking area here is small, so if you don't want to hike that extra 0.25 mile, get to the trailhead early.

The outstanding feature of this long loop hike along part of the Continental Divide Trail (CDT) is the incredible scenery. This hanging glacial valley is considered one of the most beautiful in the Indian Peaks Wilderness, justifiably famous for its awe-inspiring vistas. Devils Thumb dominates—the 600-foot granite spire that reaches to 12,150 feet as it towers above Devils Thumb Lake and gives its name to the trail, the lake, and the pass.

Dogs are not scenery hounds but they love water and plenty of it. And on this hike they will get it. With the exception of the stretch along the Continental Divide, there is constant access to water. Nonetheless, bring adequate water for your pet to keep him hydrated along the CDT stretch. Mosquito spray is an advisable precaution in the middle of the summer. In the moist creek drainages and adjoining meadows, these critters can be a nuisance.

Only do this hike if you and your dog are in top-notch physical shape. This hike is a fair-weather hike because of the long stretches above timberline, and an early start is best; be at the trailhead by 8:00 AM, or camp overnight in the vicinity of the trailhead to get an early start. Also, the hike is in Indian Peaks Wilderness, so leash regulations apply. If you choose to backpack, permits are required for overnight stays, June 1 through September 15; contact the Boulder Ranger District.

The hike is described clockwise because the uphill stretches are easier by way of the King Lake Trail. This hike can also be cut in two: one hike going to King Lake, with a second hike following the Devils Thumb Trail to Devils Thumb Pass or one of the lakes below it. You can also reach King Lake and the Continental Divide Trail via a much shorter route from Rollins Pass, but this alters the hiking experience completely.

From Hessie, begin hiking by crossing the footbridge and taking the Devils Thumb Trail, which climbs for 0.5 mile on an old road. In 0.8 mile, just before a bridge over the South Fork Middle Boulder Creek, the Devils

Creeks and mixed forests are ideal features on hikes with dogs.

Thumb Bypass Trail forks right (north). Continue on the main trail. At 1.2 miles intersect with the Lost Lake Trail and a short time later with the King Lake Trail, both on the left (west).

Turn left (west) on the King Lake Trail to begin the loop. The trail climbs steadily along the creek, and the creek and the mixed forest offer a variety of interesting adventures for your dog. Since wildlife drinks at the creek, numerous animal trails lead to it and offer tantalizing scents.

It is 4 miles to King Lake. This is the place to check the weather and decide whether you will continue with the loop. From the Continental Divide (south of the lake) until the descent to Jasper Lake, you will be above timberline.

The CDT is well marked and the 3-mile hike north to Devils Thumb Pass is on rolling tundra. The tundra is fragile, so take care to keep your dog on the trail and also restrain him if a ptarmigan appears nearby. The mother guards her chicks well and will try to lead your dog, if you don't watch out, on a merry chase away from the nest.

Devils Thumb Pass and the entire CDT ridge offer fabulous vistas in all directions. And you won't miss the magnificent Devils Thumb. From Devils Thumb Pass (12,400 feet), pick up the Devils Thumb Trail, which heads east. Drop steeply to Devils Thumb Lake and again to Jasper Lake, where the trail passes the tree line and descends into a forest. There are camping spots in the trees above the lake.

All along this stretch between the two lakes, there are numerous small ponds that will keep your dog hydrated and cool.

The last leg of the loop is a downhill hike following the Jasper Creek drainage as it makes its way to the South Fork Middle Boulder Creek. When you reach the Devils Thumb Bypass Trail, take it if the main trail is boggy. The bypass runs a bit higher on the slope of the valley, but eventually rejoins the main trail. Intersect the King Lake Trail on which you started the loop and continue downhill on the Devils Thumb Trail to the trailhead at Hessie.

Backpacking: This is a very long and strenuous day hike, so you could consider doing it as an overnight hike. Good camping sites are available along the South Fork Middle Boulder Creek drainage on the way to King Lake and again just above Jasper Lake where the trail meets timberline.

BOULDER/ LYONS

9. Ceran St. Vrain Trail and Miller Rock

Round trip: 4 miles (6 miles with climb up Miller Rock)
Hiking time: 4–5 hours
High point: 8646 feet at Miller Rock summit, 8400 at trailhead
Elevation gain: 400 feet (900 feet with climb up Miller Rock)
Best hiking time: June–October
Maps: USGS Raymond; USGS Gold Hill; Trails Illustrated Indian Peaks, Gold Hill (no. 102)
For more information: Roosevelt National Forest, Boulder Ranger District, (303) 541-2500

Getting there: On the west side of Lyons, pick up Colorado Highway 7 and drive south up South St. Vrain Creek canyon 15 miles to Colorado Highway 72. Go left (south) on Highway 72 past the town of Peaceful Valley to County Road 94 (aka Overland Road or James Canyon Drive) and turn left (east). Continue for 2 miles to Riverside Drive and turn left (north). Drive 0.5 mile to the Ceran St. Vrain trailhead, on the east side of South St. Vrain Creek. You will pass Glacier View Camp and Minnie Lake, both private, on the way to the trailhead.

This trail is named after Ceran St. Vrain (1802–1870), who was a fur trader and one of the earliest white men in Colorado. The fortress-like Miller

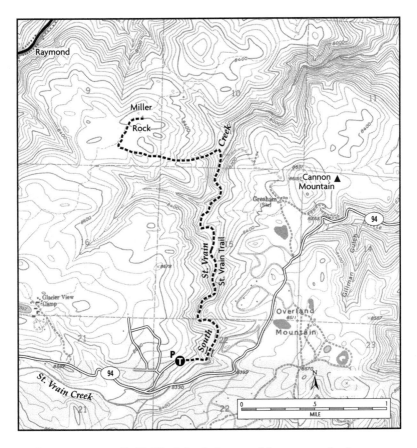

Rock, sometimes called Miller's Rock, is named for a man who is remembered either as a peaceful rancher or a habitual horse thief.

The trail follows a dense forest corridor along the creek for most of the way and is particularly attractive in the spring (early June), when the much-sought-after calypso orchid blooms abundantly in the decaying matter of the forest floor. For panoramic views, do the optional climb to Miller Rock summit, a pile of impressive boulders.

An added bonus of this hike is the soft terrain, created by the decay of pine and spruce needles over many seasons. This feature is particularly beneficial for a dog with sensitive paws or for one who is recuperating from chafed paws or injury. If this is the case, skip the steep, gravelly, and rocky ascent to Miller Rock.

The Ceran St. Vrain Trail to Miller Rock is becoming increasingly popular with mountain bikers, but on a weekday you will be alone.

View of Indian Peaks from Miller Rock

Start by crossing an old bridge over South St. Vrain Creek, then follow the easy trail into the forest and past impressive granite outcroppings. The trail gradually loses 400 feet in elevation as it parallels the creek for 1.9 miles. The farther you go, the shadier the trail becomes and the more verdant the vegetation—a lushness that is rare along the Front Range.

If your dog is a scent-hound, keep him on leash; this corridor is home to many critters, from raccoons to deer, and the plethora of scents will tempt your hound to plunge into the undergrowth to explore. This can be an adventure for you too. Watch your dog's reaction. A sudden stillness of his body and pricked ears indicate that your dog has spotted a critter, and if you follow the direction of your dog's gaze, you may also catch sight of the animal.

Waterbirds are also abundant. Look for a small, grayish, wrenlike bird called the American dipper or water ouzel. These birds live in the creek, hopping and bobbing from boulder to boulder, then suddenly plunging into the water and down to the streambed to feed on larvae. The remarkable thing about water ouzels is that they actually walk along the bottom of the stream, unaffected by the current or lack of oxygen.

The high point of the trail is at the trailhead. The trail drops 400 feet, which you have to make up on the return. Miller Rock, a towering outcropping, is reached by way of an old road encountered at 1.9 miles into the hike. The road travels away (northwest) from the creek on a rocky and steep ascent.

To climb Miller Rock, turn left (west) on the road and follow it as it climbs steeply 1 mile northwest past private property to a wider steep road. Turn right (north) and continue on a steep grade through thinning vegetation to Miller Rock. A spur takes you to the summit and if you follow it over the hill, it cuts off the corner of the climb up the gravely road. The spur rejoins the road south of Miller Rock. From here, drop down to the creek trail, turn right and return to your vehicle along the creek on terrain that rises gradually from the creek drainage.

If you forgo the Miller Rock climb and stay on the creekside trail, you will begin to gain elevation on some steep rocks. Be aware that the trail ends on a jeep road (Miller Rock Road) in 0.25 mile. So get your fill of the shaded creek and retrace your steps to the trailhead.

10. Royal Arch

Round trip: 3.2 miles
Hiking time: 4 hours
High point: 6950 feet
Elevation gain: 1300 feet
Best hiking time: April–October
Maps: USGS Eldorado Springs; Trails Illustrated Boulder, Golden (no. 100); City of Boulder Trails Map
For more information: City of Boulder Open Space and Mountain Parks Department, (303) 441-3440

Getting there: From U.S. Highway 36 in Boulder, exit onto Baseline Road heading west. Drive 1.1 miles past the intersection with Broadway to the Chautauqua Park parking lot on the left.

Royal Arch is a modest cousin of the impressive and incredible sandstone arches in Arches National Park in Utah. Yet, once at the arch, you are as close as you will get to the vertical face of the famous Flatirons unless you are a technical climber. In fact, you may see a climber negotiating a

difficult pitch. Probably the best time to reach the arch is by midmorning, to marvel as the eastern sunlight glances off the russet cliff faces.

Although Boulder permits dogs to be off-leash and under voice command, it is advisable to leash your dog before you reach the arch so that he does not venture out on the sandstone slabs—long drop-offs! And the slabs are flat enough in this area that hikers sun themselves as they watch the climbers and admire the view—unleashed dogs may be not only a nuisance, but a danger. For a thorough explanation of Boulder's regulations for dogs on trails, pick up the *Dogs on Open Space and Mountain Parks* brochure at all major trailheads or visit *www.ci.boulder.co.us/openspace/ visitor/dogs.htm.*

Boulder regulations also require that you pick up after your dog, and the city imposes very stiff penalties on violators. Plastic bags for excrement are available at dispensers at trailheads.

After parking your car, follow the main road uphill in a southerly direction from the west side of the parking lot. At 0.6 mile, the Mesa Trail

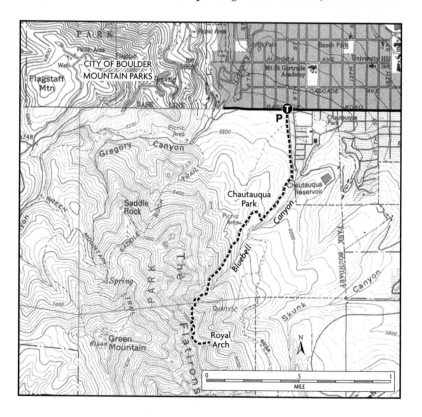

Royal Arch Trail climbs up to Boulder's famous Flatirons. (Photo by Stefan Krusze)

will veer to your left (southeast). A picnic shelter (Bluebell Shelter) and toilets are on your right. A couple of hundred feet past this area, look for a signpost pointing to the Royal Arch Trail. Bear left and begin hiking through scrub vegetation.

At a fork, keep left and ignore the faint offshoot trail. Enter a conifer forest and ascend more steeply. Throughout the hike you will catch glimpses of the five Flatirons and the Royal Arch is located on the fifth Flatiron. Switchbacks begin about 1 mile into the hike. In total, climb about a dozen switchbacks. At the top of the ridge, drop into a rocky, dry, creek drainage, then ascend steeply a short distance to the arch.

Your dog should have no trouble on the ascent if he is fit. There is a seasonal stream along the way for him to cool off and drink, and the entire hike is in a sparse but shady forest that stays cool even at midday. The trail does get rocky and bouldery, but most dogs have no problems. As a matter of fact, on one trip several dogs enjoyed scrambling up and down the stone slabs that mark some particularly steep spots on the trail. Just remember to leash up once you reach the arch.

11. Green Mountain Loop

Round trip: 5.3-mile loop
Hiking time: 5 hours
High point: 8144 feet
Elevation gain: 2250 feet
Best hiking time: April–October
Maps: USGS Eldorado Springs; Trails Illustrated Boulder, Golden (no. 100); City of Boulder Trails Map; City of Boulder Circle Hikes Guide
For more information: City of Boulder Open Space and Mountain Parks Department, (303) 441-3440

Getting there: From U.S. Highway 36 in Boulder, exit onto Baseline Road heading west. After passing Broadway, drive past Chautauqua Park turn-off to a very sharp turn in the road. Take the narrow road due south at the turn. This is the access to the parking lot for the Gregory Canyon Trail trailhead.

There are twenty peaks called Green Mountain in Colorado and this one is locally famous for its many butterflies. It is slightly behind (west of) the Flatirons, Boulder's signature mountains, and can be reached via several trails. This variation is a strenuous loop. There is a creek about halfway into the hike, but it is best to bring water along for your canine companion. It is also best to hike this loop early in the day to avoid being caught in a thunderstorm.

Boulderites love animals and this is one jurisdiction that permits dogs to hike off-leash if they are under voice command. This plus the proximity of the mountains makes hiking in Boulder's mountains very popular, especially in the Chautauqua area. For a thorough explanation of Boulder's regulations for dogs on trails, pick up the *Dogs on Open Space and Mountain Parks* brochure at all major trailheads or visit *www.ci.boulder.co.us/openspace/visitor/dogs.htm*.

Boulder regulations also require that you pick up after your dog, and

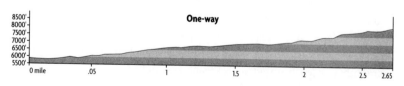

the city imposes very stiff penalties on violators. Plastic bags for excrement are available at dispensers at trailheads.

The trailhead is off Baseline Road, where it changes to Flagstaff Mountain Road. A picnic area is a short distance beyond the trailhead on the right. Start by heading south on the Gregory Canyon Trail to Green Mountain Lodge at 1.1 mile. Here, pick up the Ranger Trail to the left of the lodge and take this trail south as it switchbacks upward through woods.

If the weather turns and you want an abbreviated hike, you can bypass the summit of Green Mountain by taking the verdant E. M. Greenman Trail, which veers off to the left (east). This trail connects with the Saddle Rock Trail that takes you back down to the trailhead.

Otherwise, stay on the Ranger Trail to its intersection with the Green Mountain West Ridge Trail. Turn left (east) and scramble to the summit of Green Mountain. A bird's-eye view of the Flatirons is memorable, as are the swarms of butterflies, which are replaced in the fall with swarms of cute, red ladybugs, also called ladybird beetles.

View of Green Mountain from a field of wildflowers (Photo by Boulder Chamber of Commerce)

On the summit look for the E. M. Greenman Trail going off to the northeast. This is a shady and woodsy trail that dogs enjoy. Continue to the junction with the Saddle Rock Trail. If you stay on the E. M. Greenman Trail just past this intersection, you will come across a creek your dog will appreciate.

Otherwise, bear right (east) on the Saddle Rock Trail and descend to complete the loop.

12. South Boulder Peak and Bear Mountain

Round trip: 5.6 miles
Hiking time: 6 hours
High point: 8549 feet
Elevation gain: 3200
Best hiking time: April–October
Maps: USGS Eldorado Springs; Trail Illustrated Boulder Golden (no. 100); City of Boulder Trails Map
For more information: City of Boulder Open Space and Mountain Parks Department, (303) 441-3440

Getting there: From the intersection of Broadway and Baseline Road in Boulder, take Broadway (Colorado Highway 93) south for 4 miles to the intersection with Eldorado Springs Drive. Turn right (west) and proceed on Eldorado Springs Drive for 1.7 miles to the parking lot and information kiosk on your right (north).

This hike is as challenging as any in the high country, but Boulder is famous for rugged and tough climbs and has a population that prides itself on fostering mountaineering traditions. While many locals are drawn to the Chautauqua Park and the diehards rock-climb on the Flatirons or in nearby Eldorado Canyon, fine and strenuous hiking is readily available in south Boulder where, once you have penetrated into one of the steep canyons, there are fewer trail users. Even better, most of the hike is along a heavily shaded trail that your dog will appreciate despite the steep terrain.

Start this hike early so once you reach the ridge you won't have to scramble for cover to avoid an afternoon thunderstorm. Your dog can be off-leash if he meets Boulder's stiff voice and sight control regulations. See Boulder's *Dogs on Open Space and Mountain Parks* brochure at all major trailheads and online at *www.ci.boulder.co.us/openspace/visitor/dogs.htm.*

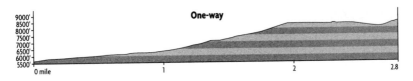

Regulations require that you pick up after your dog, and the city imposes very stiff penalties on violators. Plastic bags for excrement are available at dispensers at trailheads.

After parking your car, look for the Mesa Trail trailhead on the north side of the lot. Cross the two footbridges over South Boulder Creek. The first one is lower and offers easier access to water for your dog. Mesa Trail is wide and well maintained and is one of three access routes to the Shadow Canyon Trail that will take you to the ridgeline.

Look for the junction of the Homestead and Towhee Trails to your left (west) and take the more direct Towhee Trail. Intersect the Shadow Canyon Trail at 1.1 miles from the trailhead and turn left (west).

Shadow Canyon is dark, verdant, and has seeping springs that create puddles in several places or at least moist ground if the season is dry. The smells of the forest and the thick underbrush offer an exciting sensory experience for your dog. But this is also where the at-times-grueling climb

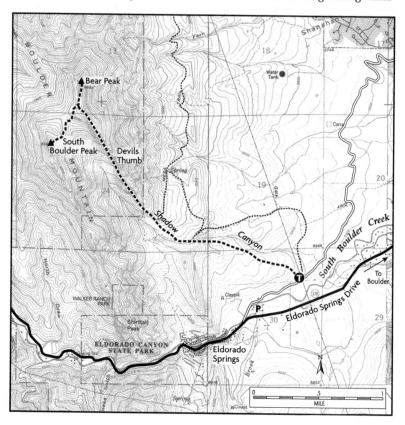

South Boulder Peak and Bear Mountain (Photo by Stefan Krusze)

begins and you gain almost all of the altitude. The trail becomes steep as it ascends through a pine and spruce forest and skirts giant sandstone rock formations. The first two are called the Matron and the Maiden. When you stop for a breather, look to your right (north) through the trees to catch a glimpse of the prominent Devils Thumb rock formation that is so striking from down in Boulder.

Once you have reached the ridge after having climbed 3000 feet in just over 2 miles, you and your pet deserve to rest and consider your options. You can head north to Bear Mountain or south to South Boulder Peak or you can summit both. The two peaks are 0.65 mile apart. The elevation gain to reach both summits once on the ridge is about 300 feet.

To reach the slightly lower Bear Mountain (8461 feet), head north (right) and follow the ridge trail north a scant 0.3 mile. The trail is broad with few rocks and without drop-offs that can worry a dog owner. The final scramble among trees and up rocks to the summit is steep but short. You will be greeted with views of the Indian Peaks and Longs Peak to the west and Boulder and the eastern plains down below.

After a rest, scramble down and retrace your steps to the saddle. Make sure your dog does not follow the familiar scents of the Shadow Canyon Trail but instead continues with you to South Boulder Peak (8549 feet). South Boulder Peak offers the same panoramic views, including a great bird's-eye view of the prominent Devils Thumb.

After feasting your eyes, head back to the saddle and return to the trailhead via Shadow Canyon and Towhee Trails. Your pet will appreciate a refreshing stop at South Boulder Creek.

13. Mesa Trail South End

One-way: 4.7 miles
Hiking time: 4 hours
High point: 6500 feet
Elevation gain: 900 feet
Best hiking time: April–June; September–October
Maps: USGS Eldorado Springs; Trail Illustrated Boulder, Golden (no. 100); City of Boulder Trails Map; brochure at trailhead
For more information: City of Boulder Open Space and Mountain Parks Department, (303) 441-3440.

Getting there: From the intersection of Broadway and Baseline Road in Boulder, take Broadway (Colorado 93) south for 4 miles to the intersection with Eldorado Springs Drive. Turn right (west) and proceed on Eldorado Springs Drive for 1.7 miles to the parking lot and information kiosk on your right (north). To reach the other end of the trail, for the recommended one-way shuttle option, you will want to leave a car at the National Center for Atmospheric Research (NCAR). From Baseline Road and Broadway head south two traffic lights to Table Mesa Drive. Turn right (west) and continue to parking at NCAR where the road ends.

This is a hike for wanderers—people and their dogs who do not necessarily want a destination. Bracketed by the ridge of mountains on the west and civilization on the east, Mesa Trail offers all sorts of detours and loops without the risk of getting lost. It has meadows, shrubbery, a couple of creeks, and a few springs that create boggy ground—features your dog will enjoy exploring. The full trail is 6.1 miles, but 4.7 miles allows for plenty of diversions and stops short of the very beautiful but crowded Chautauqua Park.

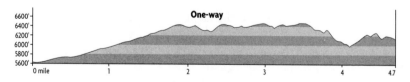

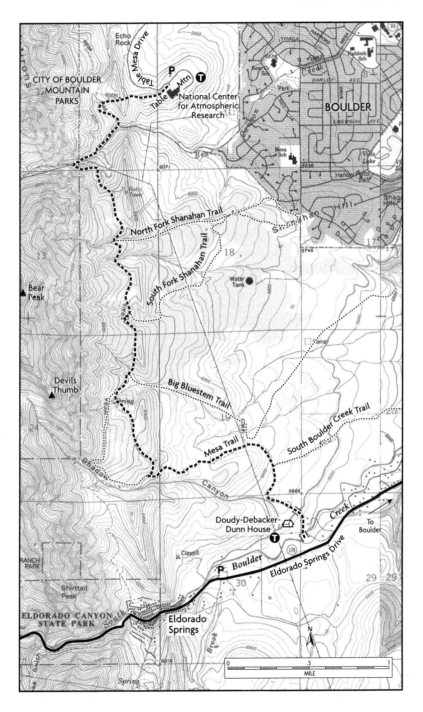

The best season for hiking the Mesa Trail starts in April with the explosion of early wildflowers such as the golden banner, wallflower, lupine, penstemon, gayfeather, and aster later on in the season. Chautauqua Meadow at the northern trailhead and the rolling meadows west of NCAR are the best-known wildflower spots. Along the trail in the spring, also look for the boulder raspberry, a showy shrub that blooms profusely with large white flowers. In the fall, the southern end of the trail in the South Boulder Creek drainage is famous for scarlet sumac and russet grasses and willows. This is also a great hike in late afternoon or early evening during the summer, allowing you and your canine companion to avoid the heat of the day. With its southern and eastern slopes, this trail can get very hot, though stands of ponderosa pine offer shade and refuge from the strong Colorado sun as the trail approaches the base of the mountains.

Mesa Trail is alive with people—and dogs—practically year-round. It is a hiker-only trail so there are no right-of-way difficulties with mountain bikers. If you want solitude or are not sure about your dog's trail behavior, pick a weekday morning to visit. If you want to show off your dog and meet other dog lovers, this hike is a 10 on weekends. The number of people and dogs rivals Denver's Washington Park, another dog mecca.

Your dog can be off-leash if he meets Boulder's stiff voice and sight control regulations. See Boulder's *Dogs on Open Space and Mountain Parks* brochure at all major trailheads and online at *www.ci.boulder.co.us/ openspace/visitor/dogs.htm*. Regulations require that you pick up after your dog, and the city imposes very stiff penalties on violators. Plastic bags for excrement are available at dispensers at trailheads. Also check for any seasonal restrictions that would require that you leash your dog.

Deer on Mesa Trail (Photo by Stefan Krusze)

After parking your car, start out on the Mesa Trail and cross two footbridges over South Boulder Creek. The first footbridge is lower and the banks are less steep, so if your dog needs a refresher at the start, this is the place. Once over the second bridge, hike straight north on a broad, car-wide trail. In a few minutes you will arrive at a junction with the Homestead and Towhee Trails, both bearing left (west). Both rejoin the Mesa Trail at Shadow Canyon and are about 0.5 mile shorter than this segment of the Mesa Trail. Nearby is the two-story stone Doudy-Debacker-Dunn House, named after the three families that occupied it. The wooden portion of the house was erected in 1858.

As it heads west, Mesa Trail begins climbing, not on switchbacks, but on a steadily rising incline. Most of the elevation gain is in this section as the trail bears northwest toward Shadow Canyon. This section epitomizes a unique ecological zone where the prairie meets the foothills and presents a tremendous variety of shrubbery, wildflowers, and grasses, as well as animal habitats. Keep an eye on your dog if he is off-leash, since it is not unusual to spot a deer or two here.

At 1.9 miles Mesa Trail splits. Each segment (west and east) is about the same length and the two merge about 0.8 mile farther north. On some maps this loop is marked as the Bluestem Loop. Whichever way you go, the loop circles a charming low-lying meadow full of flowers in the spring and soft grasses in which your dog can take a satisfying roll. Meanwhile, look west to see Devils Thumb loom high among the pines and firs.

There is also a spring near this junction that offers some pleasant refreshment for your dog. This spring is just over 2 miles from the trailhead.

Following the main Mesa Trail north brings you to another offshoot to the east (the Big Bluestem Trail) in less than a mile. Take it if you have had your fill of adventure—you will reach your starting point and the southern terminus of the Mesa Trail in 1.7 miles.

Staying the course on the Mesa Trail heading north, you reach in 0.4 mile the South Fork Shanahan Trail and North Fork Shanahan Trail, 0.5 mile farther on, both leading east into subdivisions or to connections with the Big Bluestem Trail. Continue north on the Mesa Trail and you will cross Bear Canyon Creek, where your dog may enjoy a wallow or just a refreshing drink of the clear mountain water.

The next trail intersecting on the right (east) directs you to the NCAR parking lot in 0.6 mile. Pick up your other car here if you planned a shuttle. Otherwise, return the way you came, picking up the Big Bluestem Trail to shorten the return distance.

14. Flatirons Vista and Doudy Draw

One-way: 3.7 miles, shuttle recommended
Hiking time: 3 hours
High point: 6150 feet
Elevation gain: 300-foot loss after several ups and downs
Best hiking time: April–June
Maps: USGS Eldorado Springs; Trail Illustrated Boulder, Golden (no. 100); City of Boulder Trails Map
For more information: City of Boulder Open Space and Mountain Parks Department, (303) 441-3440

Getting there: From the intersection of Broadway and Baseline Road in Boulder, take Broadway (Colorado Highway 93) south for 4 miles to the intersection with Eldorado Springs Drive. Go through the intersection and continue for another 2 miles to an obvious pullout and small parking lot on your right (west). To leave a car at the trail's other Doudy Draw trailhead for a shuttle (recommended), from the intersection of Broadway and Baseline Road in Boulder, take Broadway (Colorado Highway 93) south for 4 miles to the intersection with Eldorado Springs Drive. Turn right (west) and proceed on Eldorado Springs Drive for 1.8 miles to the parking lot and information kiosk on your left (south).

The walk across the mesa is truly a seasonal hike best done in early spring when the meadows are abloom with sego lilies, lupine, penstemon, and Indian paintbrush in quick and colorful succession. This is also a perfect evening hike on a late summer afternoon as the sun begins to set behind the tree-covered mountains, washing them and the dramatic sandstone cliffs west of Boulder.

The Doudy Draw Trail gets its name from the Doudy family that had a milk farm here. Sylvester (Andrew) Doudy was the first settler in this area. He arrived in about 1858 and, in addition to raising milk cows, also

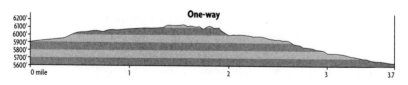

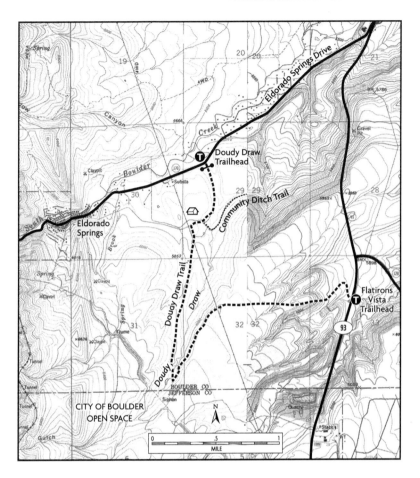

ran a sawmill and a gristmill. Remnants of the milk farm are at the picnic area near the Doudy Draw trailhead. The small building on the northeast edge of the picnic area served as a milk house. The nearby stream was diverted to the milk house to keep the canisters of fresh milk cold until they could be hauled to market.

The trail, especially toward the Doudy Draw end, is broad enough for hiker and dog to walk side by side, far removed from the bustle of the Mesa Trail (Hike 13) to the north. A good portion of the trail is also along the Doudy Draw riparian corridor, which offers shade, soft terrain, and many opportunities for your dog to get wet or lap water.

From the number of vehicles at the Doudy Draw parking lot, it appears that most hikers set out from the Doudy Draw trailhead. However,

View of Boulder Mountains from Doudy Draw trailhead

to soak in the westward views and enjoy the bonus of a downhill trail with minimal elevation gain, start at the Flatirons Vista trailhead.

Your dog can be off-leash if he meets Boulder's stiff voice and sight control regulations. See Boulder's *Dogs on Open Space and Mountain Parks* brochure at all major trailheads and online at *www.ci.boulder.co.us/ openspace/visitor/dogs.htm*. Regulations require that you pick up after your dog, and the city imposes very stiff penalties on violators. Plastic bags for excrement are available at dispensers at trailheads. Because of black bears, there are seasonal leash requirements on the Doudy Draw Trail south of Community Ditch Trail and west of the Flatirons Vista trailhead. Call Boulder's Open Space office for exact dates.

At Flatirons Vista, scramble from the road for a short distance to the mesa top, continue at a gentle uphill for 1.5 mile to the highest point of the mesa and spectacular views to the west and northwest. Next, start your descent to Doudy Draw.

At the draw, the vegetation thickens because of the nearby water. The thick brush is home to a variety of wildlife, especially deer, so keep your dog on a leash or near you as you begin to hike alongside the creek. The trail makes a sharp right turn (north) here. Look for a small pond to your left (west) where your dog can find some refreshment while you rest in the shade of a cottonwood.

Continue due north to the junction with the Community Ditch Trail, 0.5 mile before the Eldorado Springs Road. In another 0.2 mile, reach the picnic area. There are toilets here. Continue to the Doudy Draw trailhead and pass through a metal gate and then to a Boulder Open Space kiosk and the parking lot.

DENVER AND THE PLAINS

15. Platte River Greenway: Adams County

Round trip: 6.8 miles
Hiking time: 5 hours
High point: 5040 feet
Elevation gain: Negligible
Best hiking time: Year-round
Map: Denver regional street map
For more information: Adams County Parks and Community Resources, (303) 637-8001; Thornton Community Services Department, (303) 255-7831

Getting there: Take Interstate 25 north from central Denver to Interstate 76. Go east on I-76 to U.S. Highway 85, take U.S. 85 north to 104th Avenue, and turn left (west) onto 104th Avenue. Continue across a bridge over South Platte River and then a short distance to the South Platte Fishing Lakes sign and a parking lot on your right.

Once the Platte River reaches Adams County, the heavy concentration of industrial activity along its banks eases. The river curves northeast and begins its course across the flat and open prairie, giving glimpses of the broad, free-flowing river compellingly evoked by James A. Michener in

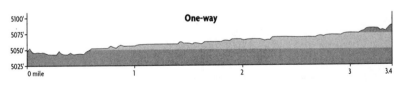

his Colorado novel *Centennial*. This area was once the agricultural center for Denver and there are still some small working farms, including
one that grows onions. The riverbanks are low and gentle, with numerous sandbars that connect to an occasional sandy beach.

The Platte River Greenway is a concrete trail that hugs the west shore
of the South Platte River. The greenway trail is complete to 104th Avenue. In 2005, a new section with three lakes stocked for fishing is set to
open north of 104th. By 2010, the trail is to be completed to Brighton, a
distance of 8 miles one-way. As this project is completed, it is worth exploring this area, since the lazy river offers low banks and easy access to

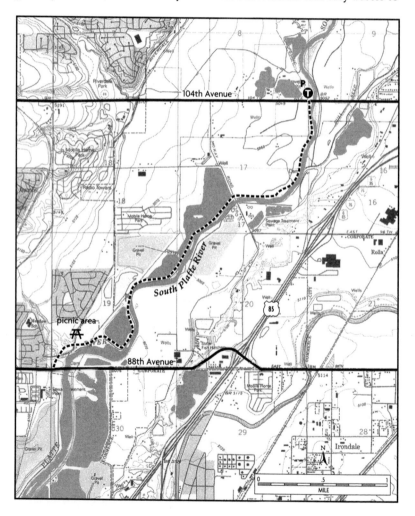

Onion field, Adams County

water for your pet. And the views southwest of the Denver metro area are breathtaking.

From 104th Avenue, wander the riverside trail south for 3.4 miles, passing several ponds and lakes that used to be gravel pits, now used for water storage. You will also pass a small farm with a corral inhabited by a flock of speckled goats. The hike ends at 88th Avenue and Colorado Boulevard in Thornton, where there is a small park and picnic and toilet facilities.

16. Sand Creek Greenway

Round trip: 2 miles
Hiking time: 1 hour
High point: 5400 feet
Elevation gain: Negligible
Best hiking time: Year-round
Maps: Denver regional street map; Sand Creek Greenway trail map
For more information: Aurora Parks and Open Space Department, (303) 739-7160; Sand Creek Regional Greenway Partnership, (303) 468-3260

Getting there: From Interstate 70 take exit 283/Chambers Road south and continue for 0.3 mile to Smith Road. Turn left (east) and drive 0.6 mile, then turn right (south) on Jasper Street. This is a narrow dirt road. Continue for 0.1 mile to an Aurora Open Space marker on the left. Park on the shoulder of the road. The road dead-ends in a couple hundred

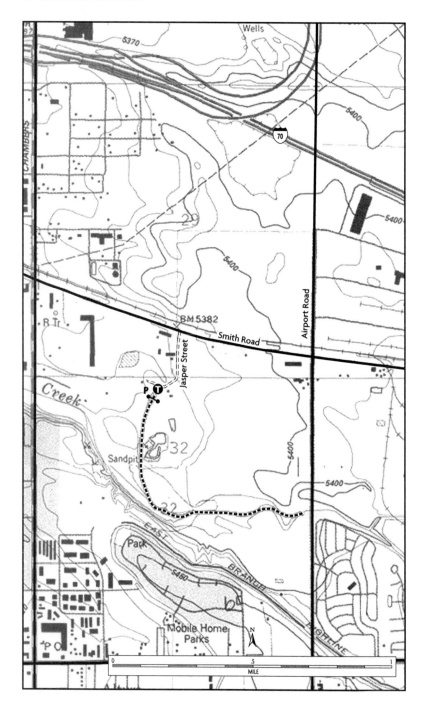

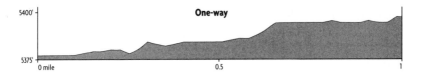

feet at Emilene's Steakhouse parking lot where there are two Conestoga wagons on display.

The Sand Creek Regional Greenway is a 13-mile greenbelt that connects the High Line Canal in Aurora at Tower Road and Colfax Avenue with the Platte River Greenway in Commerce City. This greenbelt completes a loop of 50 miles of off-street urban trails in the northeast Denver metro area.

The city of Aurora acquired the Star K Ranch, which the Sand Creek Greenway traverses, in the 1990s. The land is still mostly in its natural state and consists of meadows interspersed with stands of cottonwoods. Sand Creek flows in a deep gulch south of the trail but is accessible on several footpaths that descend into the creek gully. Your pet will enjoy exploring the slow-moving waters and the sandy bottom of this creek.

Sand Creek Greenway offers hiking opportunities in the heart of metro area.

An added plus of this close-in, urban hike is that it is largely undiscovered. And the clincher is that if you are game, you can explore the remaining 11 miles of this new greenway northwest through Aurora, Denver, and Commerce City.

Pass through the wooden gate and hike for 0.1 mile on an improved crushed gravel path. There is a bench on the right, about 200 feet from the entry gate. The gravel trail ends in the Sand Creek Trail, where you turn left (east). Continue through a meadow with several giant cottonwood trees. You can continue on the trail until you reach Airport Road and then turn around.

Or you can make a detour to the creek itself by looking to your right (south) for a distinct footpath near one of the large cottonwoods. Scamper down into the gully and in a few hundred feet you will reach the creek. It is very shallow in this area, but the water flow is constant. This is an ideal spot for your dog to get a drink of water and to frolic in the shallow, quiet stream.

17. High Line Canal: Blackmer Lake

Round trip: 4 miles
Hiking time: 1–2 hours
High point: 5500 feet
Elevation gain: 50 feet
Best hiking time: Year-round
Map: Denver regional street map
For more information: South Suburban Parks and Recreation District, (303) 798-5131

Getting there: Take exit 204/Colorado Boulevard from Interstate 25. Drive south (right) on Colorado Boulevard 3 miles to East Quincy Avenue. Turn left (east) on Quincy and drive 0.3 mile to the stop sign at South Dahlia Street. Turn right (south) and drive three blocks to the end of the road and the parking lot on the High Line Canal.

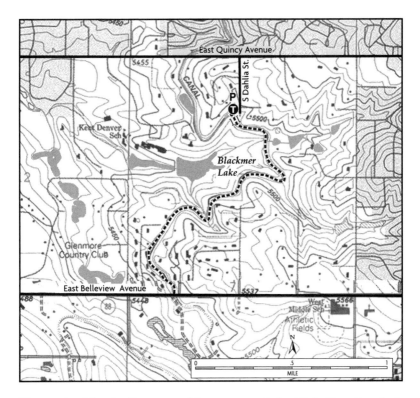

The track of land adjacent to this segment of the High Line Canal almost became the retirement home of President Dwight D. Eisenhower, whose wife, Mamie, was a Denver native. But since the president retired to Gettysburg, Pennsylvania, after his second term, the acreage became the home of the Kent Denver Day School.

When the South Suburban Parks and Recreation District came into existence, Cherry Hill Village, within whose boundaries this portion of the trail runs, contracted with the district to maintain the trail, as it does in all of Arapahoe County. The trail also serves as a maintenance road that is used by local animal control vehicles and by the Denver Water Board, which owns the canal.

This trail is very popular with hikers and bicyclists and is used by cross-country skiers after heavy snowfalls. However, if you pick an off hour, such as very early in the morning or at dusk, you can find solitude here, in the heart of the metropolitan area. This trail and hike are perfect for the older dog or for one who is recuperating from sore paws. There is only one caveat: make sure your pet stays on the trail. In the summer, the trail edges

High Line Canal in Cherry Hills

are covered in many spots with nasty burr plants. The High Line Canal also lends itself to full-moon hikes, since the trail does have open hours of 6:00 AM to 11:00 PM

The canal starts in Waterton Canyon in the foothills and flows north and east to the plains in Aurora. This section between South Dahlia Street and East Belleview Avenue in Cherry Hill Village is one of the prettiest sections of the 76-mile trail. The trail in this area remains cool even in the summer, since it is shaded by giant cottonwoods, some more than 100 years old. Once I saw a bald eagle perched on a lofty branch of one of these gnarled trees.

After parking your vehicle and leashing your dog (leashes cannot be longer than 6 feet), cross the wooden bridge over the High Line Canal. Turn left (south) and hike for 0.6 mile to the hike's centerpiece, Blackmer Lake and Blackmer Commons, a donated open space where wildlife abounds—Canada geese and mallards in the fall and winter, coyotes, foxes, and raccoons year-round.

Continue hiking while admiring the incredible panorama of the Front Range to the west. The underpass at East Belleview Avenue is in another 1 mile. In several locations, the bank of the canal levels off and your dog can get his paws wet and lap water.

Return the way you came or combine this walk with Hike 18 and continue along the canal almost another 3 miles to Orchard Road.

18. High Line Canal: Horseshoe Preserve

Round trip: 5.8 miles
Hiking time: 3 hours
High point: 5525 feet
Elevation gain: Negligible
Best hiking time: Year-round
Map: Denver regional street map
For more information: South Suburban Parks and Recreation
   District, (303) 798-5131

Getting there: Take exit 198/Orchard Road from Interstate 25. Drive west for 2.5 miles to the large gravel parking lot on the north side of East Orchard Road where it crosses the High Line Canal. The trail is open 6 AM to 11 PM and dogs must be on leashes no longer than 6 feet. Portable toilets are at the parking lot.

Since the round-trip distance on this hike is almost 6 miles, this excursion qualifies as a bona fide hike even though it is in suburbia and passes through some very expensive subdivisions. The good-sized parking lot came with the development of a subdivision called The Preserve. When the parking lot was installed, Colorado Boulevard was realigned to intercept Orchard Road a block farther east. This change is still not recorded on most maps.

The parking lot provides ample space to park, so you may enjoy this scenic and bucolic stretch of the canal trail at any time during the day and on weekends. The canal trail is composed of aggregate and is usable year round. The 1-mile portion between East Orchard Road and

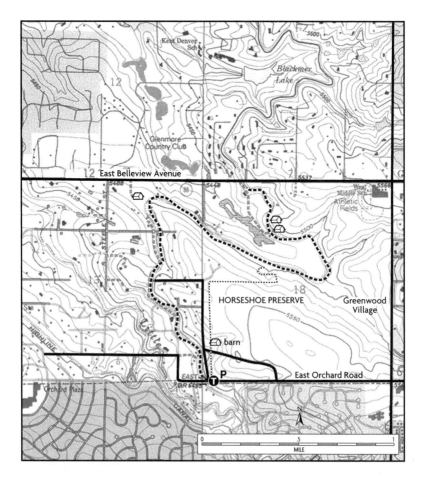

Willamette Lane offers views of the Front Range that are among the most expansive in all of the metro area. The sparsely developed character of this section of trail, once a farming community, enhances the feeling of openness. In fact, there are several small working farms less than 1 mile to the west. One of them, on Long Road, produces a bumper crop of pumpkins that are offered for sale every October.

Start from the parking lot by crossing the canal on the pedestrian portion of the small bridge and turn right (north) onto the canal trail. The highlights of this hike become immediately apparent. For the next

Opposite: Tall cottonwoods and verdant vegetation provide shaded hiking and picnicking during the summer.

1 mile, panoramic views of the Front Range extend from Mount Evans to Longs Peak. Pass an old red barn that harkens back to early settlers. Sightings of hawks, ducks, Canada geese, foxes, deer, and even coyotes are common in this area.

Since the trail serves as a levee, you are always slightly higher than the sloping land to the west and so the Front Range views continue. The canal also has sloping banks and short vegetation so there are numerous gentle descents to the canal for your dog to enjoy. Just before you reach Willamette Lane, there is a bench where you can sit down to rest or enjoy the view. At 1 mile, the canal trail crosses narrow Willamette Lane, a rural street that provides restricted access to a horse farm and another home on the east side of the canal where the lane dead-ends. Past Willamette there are two horse farms on the west side of the canal as well as several houses as the canal approaches East Belleview Avenue. In the next 0.25 mile, traffic noise intrudes on the silence, but the trail and canal veer to the southeast to form a 1.5-mile-long, sweeping curve around a wildlife preserve commonly called the Horseshoe Preserve, owned by Greenwood Village. Two benches are located in this area and offer prime places to sit quietly for sighting birds and other wildlife.

At the start of the curve, you can see split-rail fencing across the canal that marks the equestrian trail that was completed in 2003. A few hundred feet past a mile marker that says "South Suburban 6.5" there is an equestrian bridge that crosses the canal and leads to the Greenwood Village trail system.

Once past the equestrian bridge, the canal trail loops back west then north and passes a subdivision of luxury townhomes on the east side of the canal. Turn around at the underpass at East Belleview Avenue or extend your hike along the canal to Blackmer Lake (Hike 17).

If you want to take 1 mile off the round-trip distance, or simply want a different way back to your car, cross the canal at the equestrian bridge. Immediately make a right (south) and follow the equestrian trail. The trail turns east, then south, then west, to go around three houses. It emerges at the intersection of Garden Avenue where South Colorado Boulevard dead-ends. The trail follows the east side of South Colorado Boulevard for 0.5 mile, then crosses it where the street touches the east bank of the High Line Canal. The trail continues for a few hundred feet along the east side of the canal before emerging at the north end of the parking lot at East Orchard Road.

19. Cherry Creek State Park

Round trip: 1.5 miles
Hiking time: Varies
High point: 5660 feet
Elevation gain: Negligible
Best hiking time: Year-round
For more information: Cherry Creek State Park, (303) 699-3860

Getting there: From Interstate 225, take Parker Road south to Orchard Road and turn right (west). From Orchard Road, take the first right turn into the parking area. Self-pay parking is $6 daily; if you plan to visit this off-leash area often, you may want to purchase the $58 annual pass.

The Cherry Creek State Park off-leash area is truly a dog heaven. It is arguably the best place in metro Denver for your dog to run off-leash with the blessing of animal-control officers. The extra-wide and surprisingly long off-leash area offers a variety of recreational opportunities. Besides running through the tall grass along the trail, your dog can take a quick dip in Cherry

Cherry Creek offers numerous opportunities for an off-leash frolic.

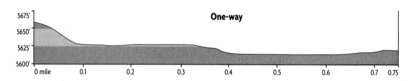

Creek or paddle along for a while and then join you under tall cotton-woods for a rest and a shady respite from the hot Colorado sun. The only requirement for enjoying this off-leash canine paradise is that your dog must be voice or sight trained. The off-leash area stretches for more than a mile as it runs south along Cherry Creek, which flows slowly here and has a broad, rock-free, sandy bottom. Dogs seem to know they are in heaven and behave accordingly.

Owners who might be less active than their pets can sit at one of two benches strategically placed in the shade of cottonwoods. While not watching Rover, you can savor the fine vistas of the Front Range.

The training area is marked by signs and extends to the right (north)

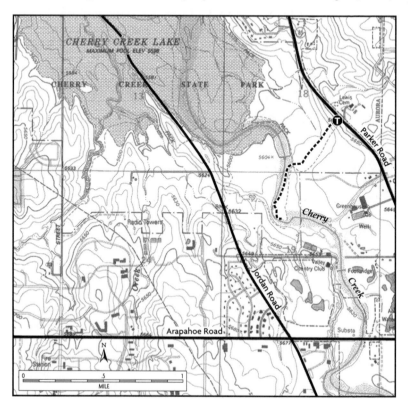

to a rail fence. A packed-dirt jeep road leads southwest through the middle of the area for 0.3 mile. Wetlands of cattails and willows are to the west and these are off-limits to your dog and are clearly marked. The jeep road ends at the bank of Cherry Creek.

For a short, pleasant walk, take a narrow trail left (south) that follows the creek. There is a bench here under a cottonwood, which grows at a strange acute angle. Nearby is one of several low access points to the creek. The shallow bank spills over a flat, sandy bottom. This is a great place for a dog to retrieve a thrown ball or a Frisbee while splashing in shallow water.

Continue for another 0.4 mile until the trail crosses the paved path that runs south to north through the park. The park boundary is a few dozen feet on the south side of the paved path. A bench offers great Front Range views. Return the way you came, but allow your dog time for another frolic in the water.

20. Castlewood Canyon State Park

Round trip: 5.6-mile loop
Hiking time: 5 hours
High point: 6650 feet
Elevation gain: 600 feet
Best hiking time: April–May; September–October
Map: Castlewood Canyon trail map available at entry station
For more information: Castlewood Canyon State Park, (303) 688-5242

Getting there: Take Interstate 25 south from Denver or north from Colorado Springs to exit 182 at Castle Rock. Turn east on Colorado Highway 86 and go 6 miles to Franktown. Turn south on Colorado Highway 83 (South Parker Road) and drive 5 miles south to the park entrance on your right. Drive to the parking lot and picnic area at Canyon Point. The park is open 8:00 AM to 9:00 PM and dogs must be leashed. Day use costs $5 and an annual pass costs $55.

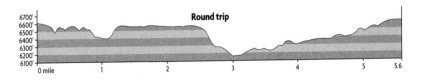

As with the Grand Canyon but on a much smaller and much less grand scale, you don't realize it's there until you have crossed the rolling plain and are staring speechless on the edge of a deep fissure that was carved by water eroding rock over the millennia. In the case of Castlewood Canyon, the erosion was by Cherry Creek, which is famous as the stream in which gold was discovered in 1858.

Castlewood Canyon State Park is in eastern Douglas County. Denver is downstream and ever since Colorado's settlement, Cherry Creek floods plagued the city. Thus, the first use that was made of the canyon was in 1889–1890 when a dam was built across the canyon's western outlet to control water flow and offer irrigation on the dry plains. Then, after torrential rains on August 3, 1933, the dam collapsed and a 15-foot-high wall of water flooded Denver, killing two people and causing extensive damage. Subsequent floods led to the eventual construction of the Cherry

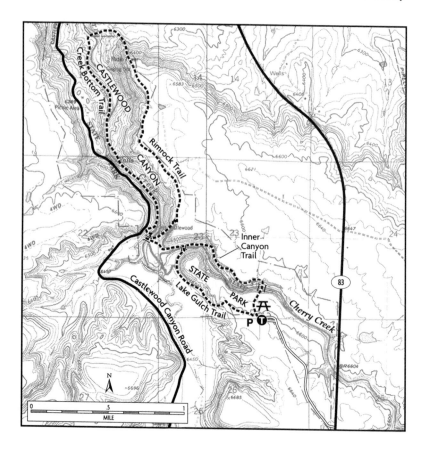

Creek Dam much farther downstream in what is now Aurora. The Castlewood Canyon dam was never rebuilt and Castlewood Canyon became a state park in 1980.

Why hike Castlewood Canyon? For one, it is great in early spring when the mountains are still knee-deep in snow and you and your dog are itching for some scrambling. There are also 13 miles of trails for exploring in the canyon, detailed in the park brochure. The hike described here is a loop consisting of three canyon-bottom trails and the long upper-rim trail. Ruins of the original dam can be examined from the lower trails.

From the northwest edge of the parking lot, follow signs for the Inner Canyon Trail. Descend into the canyon on a series of steps hewn from rock. Once at the bottom of the canyon, cross Cherry Creek on a wooden plank bridge and turn left to follow the creek

Canyon walls carved by Cherry Creek

downstream to the ruins of the old dam, 1.6 miles from the trailhead. The main shaft of the old dam is across the creek from you.

Turn around and look for the start of the Rimrock Trail. You will climb some 300 feet out of the canyon. Once on top, turn left and continue along the rim to one of several overlooks that provide a view down into the canyon and across the plains to the west and the mountains of the Front Range.

Follow the Rimrock Trail for just over 2 miles to its end and descend again into the canyon on the Creek Bottom Trail. This trail turns southeast as it continues along the west side of Cherry Creek until you reach the dam ruins. Cross the creek and hike Inner Canyon Trail a short way to another bridge across the creek. Turn right and pick up the Lake Gulch Trail, which will take you back to Canyon Point in 0.8 mile.

DENVER FOOTHILLS

21. Windy Peak

Round trip: 4.5-mile loop
Hiking time: 4 hours
High point: 9141 feet
Elevation gain: 1000 feet
Best hiking time: May–June; September–October
Maps: USGS Black Hawk; Trail Illustrated Boulder, Golden (no. 100); park brochure available at entrance station and visitors center
For more information: Golden Gate Canyon State Park, (303) 582-3707

Getting there: From Golden (west of Denver), drive 3.5 miles north on U.S. Highway 6 to its intersection with Colorado Highway 93 and Colorado Highway 58. Continue north on Colorado Highway 93 toward Boulder. In 1 mile, look for the sign for Golden Gate Canyon State Park. Turn left (west) onto the park access road and drive into the foothills for 13 miles on the twisting and climbing paved road. Once you reach the park, turn right and continue to the visitors center on the right. Pay the day-use fee at the visitors center or at the park's entrance station. Seasonal passes are also available. From the visitors center, drive 2.2 miles to the Burro Trail trailhead parking lot on the left. This is a small parking lot, accommodating about a dozen cars. There are toilets here and the Bridge Creek picnic area is nearby.

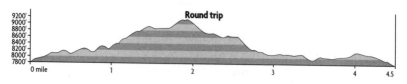

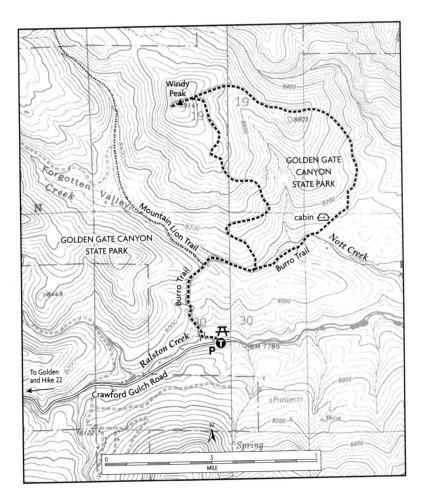

Although no gold was found in what is today Golden Gate Canyon State Park, the Golden Gate Canyon Road was built to reach the gold bonanza camps in Black Hawk and Central City, southwest of here. In subsequent decades, the land was used for farming and ranching. The state began acquiring land for the park in 1960. Today, 14,000 acres of meadows, forests, and peaks offer a backcountry hiking, backpacking, and camping getaway only 30 miles from Denver. A series of interconnected mountain trails make for a fresh experience on each visit. Hiking, biking, and horseback riding are permitted and certain trails are restricted to hikers only. Your pet companion must be leashed.

There are twelve interconnected trails in the park, each named after an animal and marked with the animal's footprint. The background shape of the trail marker indicates the difficulty of the trail. Circles denote easy trails, squares are moderate, and diamonds mark the difficult trails. Trailheads with parking areas are easily accessible from the main roads in the park. The rustic visitors center has water, restrooms, and exhibits of local fauna and flora, as well as detailed maps of the park and its environs.

One of the most interesting hikers-only trails is the difficult Burro Trail, which climbs through meadows and forests to Windy Peak (9141 feet). For added hiking interest, you can visit the peak via a loop trip starting on the Burro Trail.

From the parking area, proceed in a northerly direction on the Burro Trail. Bear right at the intersection of the Mountain Lion Trail and again at the intersection with the south loop of the Burro Trail (this is your return route).

At about 1 mile, reach Nott Creek where your canine companion can find refreshment, and continue on the trail through a meadow to a homesteader's cabin scenically positioned at the head of a small pond. Return to the Burro Trail and proceed in a northwesterly direction through a mixed forest to Windy Peak. A short scramble over rocks will put you on the peak, which offers vistas of the Continental Divide.

Descend from the peak and look for a trail also marked Burro Trail forking to the right (south). At 3.5 miles you will reach the start of the loop. Turn right to retrace your steps to your car.

Cabin on the trail to Windy Peak

22. Frazer Meadow

Round trip: 4.5 miles
Hiking time: 4 hours
High point: 9200 feet
Elevation gain: 1000 feet
Best hiking time: May–June; September–October
Maps: USGS Black Hawk; Trails Illustrated Boulder, Golden (no. 100);
   park brochure available at entrance station and visitors center
For more information: Golden Gate Canyon State Park, (303) 582-3707

Getting there: From Golden (west of Denver), drive 3.5 miles north on U.S. Highway 6 to its intersection with Colorado Highway 93 and Colorado Highway 58. Continue north on Colorado Highway 93 toward Boulder. In 1 mile, look for the sign for Golden Gate Canyon State Park. Turn left (west) onto the park access road and drive into the foothills for 13 miles on the twisting and climbing paved road. Once you reach the park, turn right and continue to the visitors center on the right. Pay the day-use fee at the visitors center or at the park's entrance station. Seasonal passes are also available. From the visitors center, drive for 0.5 mile to the Frazer Meadow trailhead parking lot on the left. This is a small parking lot, accommodating about a dozen cars. There are also toilets here.

Golden Gate Canyon State Park got its name from Golden Gate City, which was located at the mouth of Tucker Gulch that led to the gold fields of Black Hawk and Central City. The two former mining towns, now popular as limited-stakes gambling destinations, are southwest of the park.

Situated 30 miles from Denver, Golden Gate Canyon State Park offers 14,000 acres of conifer forest, rocky peaks, mountain splendor, and aspen-filled meadows. There are twelve trails in the park, each named after an animal and marked with the animal's footprint. The background shape of the trail marker indicates the difficulty of the trail. Circles denote easy trails, squares are moderate, and diamonds mark the difficult trails. Trailheads

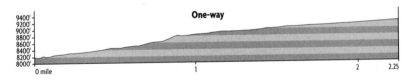

with parking areas are easily accessible from the main roads in the park. The pleasant visitors center has water, restrooms, and exhibits of local fauna and flora, as well as detailed maps of the park and its environs.

From the Fraser Meadow trailhead, hike the well-maintained trail following and crossing Ralston Creek five times on sturdy footbridges. You will be on Horseshoe Trail, which is clearly and frequently marked with a sign of a horseshoe. Cross a bridge and continue slowly climbing up the aspen-covered hillside. Cross the creek again and then a third time. You will be hiking through stands of aspen, which make this hike particularly pleasant in September when aspen glow with brilliant orange-yellow. Eventually the forest thins and you pass through several small meadows.

Frazer Meadow has the ruins of an old homesteading cabin right off the trail. The east side of the meadow is marshy and is famous for wild

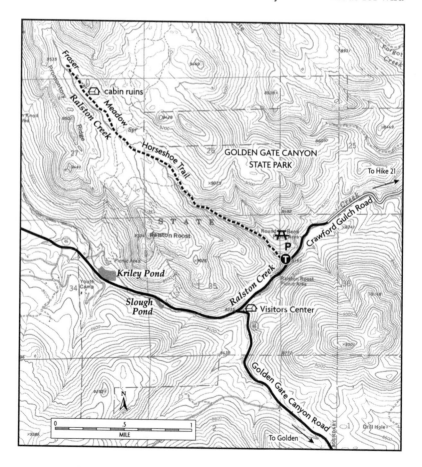

On the trail to Frazer Meadow

iris and shooting stars in the spring. There is no creek at the meadow, so bring your pet's water dish and water.

Return the way you came.

23. Beaver Brook Trail and Braille Nature Trail

Round trip: 3.6 miles
Hiking time: 3 hours
High point: 7400 feet
Elevation gain: 800 feet
Best hiking time: May–June; September–October
Maps: USGS Evergreen; Trails Illustrated Boulder, Golden (no. 100)
For more information: Denver Parks and Recreation Department, (720) 913-0739; Mountain Parks Information, (303) 697-4545

Getting there: Take Interstate 70 west from Denver to the Chief Hosa exit (exit 253). At the bottom of the ramp turn right and continue as the road turns into Stapleton Drive and curves northwest. Follow Stapleton Drive for 1 mile and bear left at a fork that leads to two parking lots. Park in either lot, although the bottom lot is closer to the trailhead.

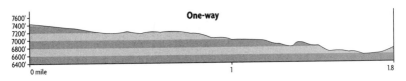

The Beaver Brook Trail extends for 8.65 miles through open space owned by the City and County of Denver in Genesee Park and on Lookout Mountain. Constructed from 1917 to 1919 with the help of the Colorado Mountain Club, the trail hugs the south rim of Clear Creek Canyon.

Because the area has been protected from development for almost 100 years, Beaver Brook Trail offers a unique primitive backcountry hiking experience in the metropolitan area. The entire trail is a long, strenuous trip with an exposed talus field around Lookout Mountain at the east

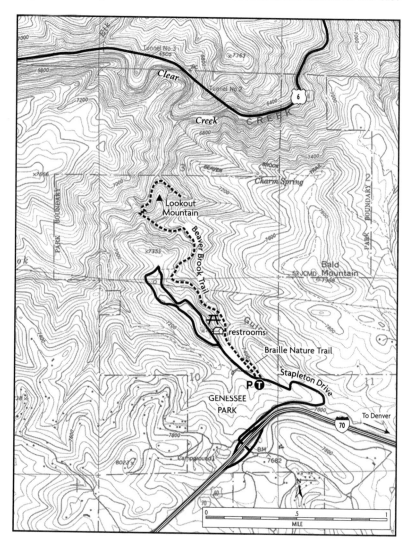

Forest meadow at Beaver Brook

end. But the west end of the trail makes for a less difficult but nonetheless challenging hike since all of the elevation gain is on the way back, when you and your pet are tired. An added feature of this hike is the short Braille Nature Trail, which would be an interesting hiking experience for a nonsighted person with a seeing-eye dog.

Start at the clearly marked trailhead for the Braille Nature Trail. The next 0.3 mile is a gradual descent along a trail that has a sturdy vinyl-coated cable strung from waist-high posts. At regularly spaced intervals, tablets written in Braille explain the surrounding ecosystem. There are also several large trail signs explaining how sighted hikers might duplicate the sensory experiences on which nonsighted hikers depend.

The Braille Nature Trail turns left and reverses its climb back to the trailhead near a flat small meadow where there are picnic tables and toilet facilities. Pick up the Beaver Brook Trail where the Braille Nature Trail turns.

Go down a series of uneven slab rock steps and cross a footbridge over a stagnant seasonal creek. The narrow trail takes off from there, descending rapidly into Bear Gulch. The bottom of the gulch is down the drop-off to your right. Occasional tree-mounted trail makers with "BB" on them lead you down farther into the gulch. When the grade becomes steeper, additional stone steps again take you downward. Your destination is a grassy pleasant place where the trail reaches Beaver Brook.

This picturesque terminus is delightful in spring and early summer when it is abloom with wildflowers. This small creek flows north for less than 0.25 mile to empty into the large Clear Creek. Have lunch at Beaver Brook while your pet enjoys the water and then return the way you came. Once you reach the Braille Nature Trail, take the right-hand loop segment to the trailhead.

Or you can continue on the Beaver Brook Trail as time and stamina permit. Once the trail leaves Beaver Brook it ascends to traverse the south rim of Clear Creek Canyon. Here the going is precipitous as you look far down into the canyon at Clear Creek and U.S. Highway 6. This part of the trail is for the agile, sure-footed hiker. The trail then continues east around Lookout Mountain where handhold scrambles over outcrops are necessary. The east-end trailhead is at Windy Saddle, which can be reached from U.S. Highway 6 in Golden. If you decide to hike the entire length of the Beaver Brook Trail, do so as a shuttle since the round trip distance is 18 miles, much too long to hike in one day, especially with a dog. Also, start at the Braille Nature Trail trailhead to make the steep and exposed segment near Windy Saddle a somewhat easier downhill.

24. Apex Trail/Enchanted Forest

Round trip: 4.7 miles
Hiking time: 4 hours
High point: 7550 feet
Elevation gain: 1350 feet
Best hiking time: April–May; September–October
Maps: USGS Morrison; Trails Illustrated Boulder, Golden (no. 100); Jefferson County Open Space brochure available at trailhead
For more information: Jefferson County Open Space, (303) 271-5925

Getting there: From Denver, take Interstate 70 west to exit 259/Morrison. There is a stoplight at the bottom of the ramp. Turn right

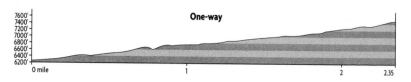

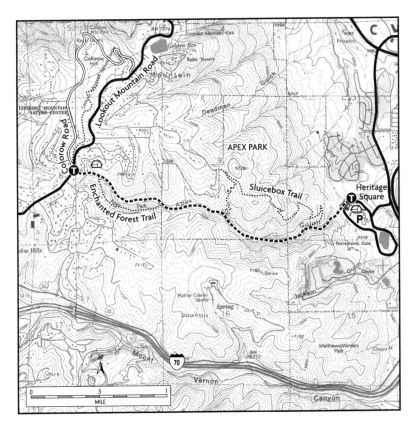

(north) onto U.S. Highway 40. Drive 1 mile to the entrance to Heritage Square on the left. Turn into the drive leading to the frontier-style shopping mall, then turn right (north) into the lower parking lot. Drive to the northwest corner of the parking lot where there is a large brown-and-beige Jefferson County Open Space sign marking the trailhead. A portable toilet, hidden by a wooden stockade, is nearby.

This hike lends itself to a car shuttle, especially if your aim is a conditioning hike up a steep slope in tough terrain. To leave a car at the northwest trailhead, drive west from Denver on Interstate 70 and take exit 256/Lookout Mountain. At the top of the ramp, turn left (west) on the service road. After 1.5 miles turn right (north) onto Lookout Mountain Road. Drive another 1.5 miles to a sign that says the Nature Center is to the left. Park just short of the sign at the intersection with Crestvue Drive. The shoulder on both sides of the road is wide and can accommodate several cars. The trailhead to the Apex Trail is about 30 feet south of the sign and is clearly marked.

It's steep. It's close to the metro area. Bikers love it on weekends. Yet it has a tumbling creek and an enchanting and shady side trail your pet will love. Apex Trail is an early spring conditioning climb; hiking this trail early in the season will test your and your dog's stamina for a climb in the high country when the snow finally melts. The main trail is gravelly and narrow so this is also a good place to toughen your dog's paws or to determine if your dog likes this type of rugged hiking. Apex Trail is best attempted on a weekday, and an early start gets you up the trail before bikers arrive.

Located in Golden, Apex Trail climbs steeply up Lookout Mountain. Back in the 1870s, this trail was a toll road to the rich gold mines in Black Hawk and Central City. Today, signs along the trail recall its past. One sign announces that the owner of a wagon drawn by a single team of horses, mules, or oxen had to pay a 60-cent toll, while 1 cent was charged for every head of sheep passing along the toll road.

From the trailhead, take the paved trail west, cross the wooden bridge and start climbing. The trail runs along Apex Creek and there are many places where the creek bank is low and your pet can wet his paws and lap water.

Keep going straight up past the Sluicebox Trail turnoff on your right in 1.5 miles. Continue going up to the turnoff for the Enchanted Forest Trail on your left at 1.8 miles, turn left (south) here. You will enter a shaded,

Apex Trail offers an early-season conditioning hike.

tranquil oasis with soft, mossy ground, covered with ferns. This is a great place to rest and to have lunch under tall ponderosa pines. If your dog is hot and panting from the grueling climb, rest here in the shade.

The Enchanted Forest Trail is a 0.7-mile half loop that returns to the main trail. Here you have a choice. You can continue climbing west past houses to Lookout Mountain Road, 0.3 mile more. Or, you can turn east and descend Apex Trail back to Heritage Square.

If you are only interested in a conditioning climb or have bad knees, you can arrange to be picked up at the trailhead marker on the right side of Lookout Mountain Road.

25. Bear Creek Trail through Four Parks

One-way: 6.1 miles, shuttle recommended
Hiking time: 5–6 hours
High point: 7400 feet at Panorama Point
Elevation gain: 1300 feet
Best hiking time: May–September
Maps: USGS Evergreen; Trails Illustrated Boulder, Golden (no. 100); Jefferson County Open Space trails brochure available at Lair o' the Bear Park
For more information: Jefferson County Open Space, (303) 271-5925; Denver Parks and Recreation Department, (720) 913-0739; Mountain Parks Information, (303) 697-4545

Getting there: From C-470 take the Morrison Road exit and drive west to the town of Morrison. Continue through town and on the west edge of town pick up Colorado Highway 74. Continue west for 4 miles to the Lair o' the Bear Park entrance on the left. Leave a car here for a car shuttle.

Return to Colorado Highway 74, turn left (west), and continue to the town of Kittredge. In the middle of town, turn left (south) on Myers Gulch Road. Continue to Pence Park (clearly marked) on the right and park here.

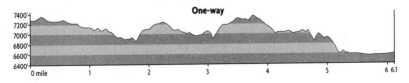

In 1909, the City and County of Denver began accumulating land in the mountains to protect its water supply. Today, the Denver Mountain Park system consists of thirty-one named parks and sixteen unnamed parks that total about 14,000 acres of mountain and foothills land. The Bear Creek Trail passes through three of these city-owned parks and ends in Lair o' the Bear, a Jefferson County Open Space park.

The trail has several access points as it winds north through the foothills. The hike described here begins in Pence Park in Kittredge, passes

Bear Creek Trail is popular with dogs and owners.

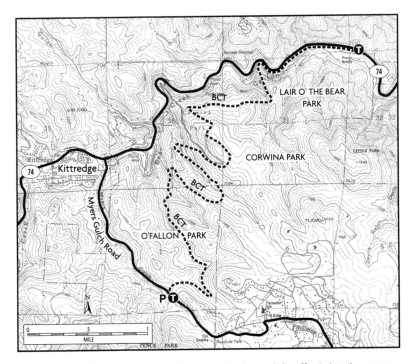

through O'Fallon Park, then Corwina Park, and finally joins its namesake, Bear Creek, as the trail enters the west end of Lair o' the Bear Park.

Your reward comes about halfway through the hike when you savor the fantastic view of Mount Evans from Panorama Point. Your patient canine companion has to wait until the last segment of the hike for his reward—paws planted in a cooling stream and a long, satisfying lap of mountain water. Bring along extra water so that your dog can be well hydrated on this long hike.

Look for the Bear Creek Trail (BCT) trailhead on the north end of the parking lot at Pence Park. Almost immediately, cross Myers Gulch Road, and pick up the trail that is marked with posts and a BCT symbol. In about 1 mile the trail intersects the Meadow View Loop trail system, which consists of several trails. The loop is to the west of the Bear Creek Trail and will intersect with Bear Creek Trail again. At each intersection bear right (east).

In 2.75 miles intersect with the Panorama Point Trail, heading southeast from its trailhead in Corwina Park. The Panorama Point Trail joins the Bear Creek Trail for 0.25 mile. Next, leave the Bear Creek Trail and follow the switchbacks to Panorama Point on the Panorama Point Trail. Panorama Point is a great place for lunch and for enjoying the sweeping vista.

Instead of retracing your steps to pick up Bear Creek Trail again, bushwhack due north a few hundred feet down from Panorama Point to the Bear Creek Trail. Turn right and proceed on the trail for another 1 mile to the intersection with Bear Creek. Here, the Bear Creek Trail begins to run alongside the Creekside Trail in Lair o' the Bear Park.

This is the segment of the hike where your patient dog will get his reward. The creek, which is on your right, has gently sloping banks, which enable your dog to wallow and get his paws wet as well as to satisfy his thirst. Several rivulets flowing to Bear Creek across the trail also afford water access for your pet.

A small, grayish, wrenlike bird called the American dipper or water ouzel resides in this section of the creek. Try to spot one and watch it for a moment. These birds hop and bob among the rocks along the stream, then suddenly plunge into the water for a meal. Dippers are rather remarkable in that they actually walk along the bottom of the stream, seemingly oblivious to the current, as they feed on the insect larvae.

Continue for the last 1.1 on the Creekside Trail to the parking lot on your left and your car. Then return to pick up the other vehicle at Pence Park.

26. Elk Meadow Off-Leash Area and Bergen Peak

Round trip: 7.8 miles
Hiking time: 6 hours
High point: 9708 feet
Elevation gain: 2188 feet
Best hiking time: June–October
Maps: USGS Evergreen; Trails Illustrated Boulder, Golden (no. 100); Jefferson County Open Space trails brochure available at the trailhead
For more information: Jefferson County Open Space, (303) 271-5925; Denver Parks and Recreation Department, (720) 913-0739; Mountain Parks Information, (303) 697-4545; Colorado Department of Natural Resources, Division of Wildlife, (303) 297-1192

Getting there: From Interstate 70, take exit 252/Evergreen and drive for 6 miles on Evergreen Parkway (Colorado Highway 74) to Stage Coach

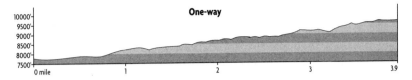

Boulevard. Turn right (west) and drive for 1.2 miles to the Elk Meadow Park parking lot on the right (north).

Jefferson County's Elk Meadow Park was homesteaded in the 1860s. Over the years, the homesteads were consolidated into a ranch that by the 1940s encompassed 1140 acres, now all park land. Rancher Darst Buchanan pastured a herd of purebred Hereford cattle on the property. In 1949, Texan Cole Means purchased the ranch as a summer pasture for his Texas herd and in 1977 the Jefferson County Open Space program acquired the land.

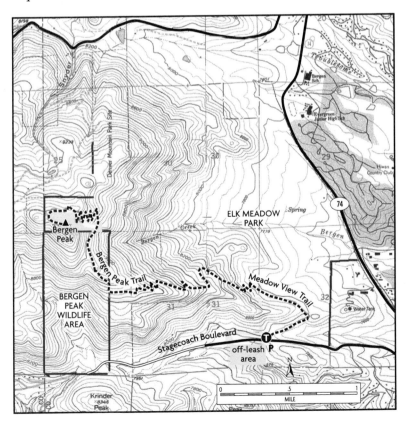

The park offers a diversity of ecosystems, from rolling meadows to ponderosa pine forests to rocky summits covered with Douglas fir and scattered aspen groves. A web of interconnected trails leads from Elk Meadow into adjacent public lands owned by both the City and County of Denver and the state. The park has also set aside several acres of off-leash terrain.

The off-leash area is on the south side of Stage Coach Boulevard. The area consists of a tall-grass meadow that is bisected by a trail, a stand of aspen on the south side of the meadow, and a small mountain stream that descends rather steeply into a gulch to the park boundary that is clearly marked by fences and signs.

The arduous climb up Bergen Peak begins in Elk Meadow, crosses quickly into Denver-owned land, cuts diagonally across the Colorado Division of Wildlife–managed Bergen Peak Wildlife Area to return to Denver-owned land for the climb up to Bergen Peak.

In all three jurisdictions, leash regulations are in effect, and in early spring the Bergen Peak Wildlife Area may be temporarily off-limits to dogs during wildlife breeding. So if you hike in months different from those recommended, check with state authorities about access.

Off-leash area in Elk Meadow

To reach the off-leash area, first cross Stage Coach Boulevard carefully. Signs and a narrow trail lead to the dog-training area 0.25 mile to the west. The trail follows the road until it reaches the meadow and a trail that branches off to the left.

Let Rover romp down the trail through the meadow and into the trees where a small creek crosses the trail. Farther along, the trail leaves the creek, which descends into a gully. The trail ends in 0.3 mile at a wire fence that designates private land beyond. Return the way you came.

To climb Bergen Peak, find the trailhead at the west side of the parking lot for the Meadow View

Trail, one of the main trails in Elk Meadow Park. Follow the trail northeast, then northwest on a wide curve as it skirts a large open meadow. The terrain rises moderately as you head toward the Bergen Peak Trail at 1 mile.

Bear left (west) at the sign for the Bergen Peak Trail and enter the ponderosa pine forest. The trail heads due west and alternates between sharp, tight switchbacks and more-moderate uphill as it passes from city-owned to state-owned land. The trail bears northwest diagonally across the rising terrain to the southeast slope of Bergen Peak.

From here, the trail begins a sharp uphill climb around the east, then the north slope of the mountain before heading west and then turning sharply east to reach the rocky summit. All along the climb, a forest of lodgepole pine and Douglas fir offers shade and relatively soft ground your dog's paws will appreciate.

From the summit, the view is over the foothills to the plains in the east, and across intervening canyons to the Continental Divide in the west.

Return the way you came.

27. Plymouth Mountain

Round trip: 6.4-mile loop
Hiking time: 5–6 hours
High point: 7295 feet
Elevation gain: 1300 feet
Best hiking time: April–May; September–October
Maps: USGS Indian Hills; Trails Illustrated Boulder, Golden (no.
   100); Jefferson County Open Space trails brochure
For more information: Jefferson County Open Space, (303) 271-5925

Getting there: From Colorado 470, exit at Wadsworth Avenue southbound. Continue about 3 miles to South Deer Creek Canyon Road (almost directly across from entrance to Chatfield State Park). Turn right (west) and continue for 6.2 miles to Grizzly Drive on your left. Turn onto Grizzly Drive and continue 0.25 mile to the parking lot.

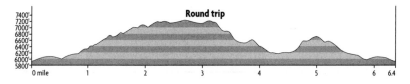

Deer Creek Canyon Park is one of Jefferson County's open space acquisitions in the foothills of the Front Range. The program to acquire former ranchland and historic sites began in 1972. John Williamson, who came from Plymouth, England, in 1872, once homesteaded a portion of the park. He is credited with naming Plymouth Creek and Plymouth Mountain, the destination of this hike.

Because this open space has seven interconnected trails, you have a variety of options for hiking depending on your stamina and on the weather. East- and south-facing slopes can get very hot in the summer, so the best hiking time is in the spring and fall, when the groves of Gamble (scrub) oak turn a burnished orange.

This loop hike begins at the parking lot at the Plymouth Creek Trail trailhead. Ascend southwest on rolling terrain that is sandy and desertlike. As the trail nears Plymouth Creek and drops into the gulch, the landscape changes to a mixed forest. Cross the creek on a sturdy bridge. Nearby are shallow pools of water between boulders where your dog can get refreshed.

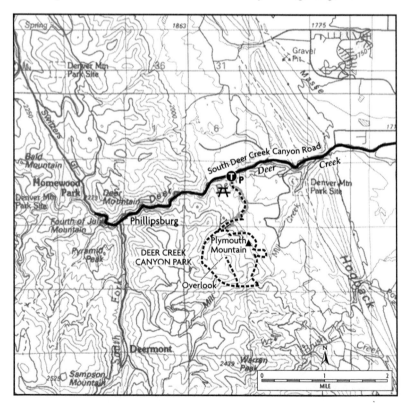

View from the summit of Plymouth Mountain

The Meadowlark Trail (Hike 28) bears off to the right but continue left (west) on the Plymouth Creek Trail. This is a steep and rocky climb following the creek, but it is shaded. In another 0.4 mile reach the intersection with the Plymouth Mountain Trail. This trail creates a circle around Plymouth Mountain, so it does not matter which way you do the circle. Following the circle counterclockwise will get most of the elevation gain out of the way early in the hike.

Continuing slightly right (counterclockwise), still in a forest setting, you will reach a junction with the Golden Eagle Trail off to your right in 0.4 mile. Continue on the Plymouth Mountain Trail for another 0.5 mile, then turn left for the short uphill 0.4-mile segment to the top of Plymouth Mountain and a beautiful 360-degree summit view.

After a rest and lunch, descend the way you came and turn left on the Plymouth Mountain Trail to return to the creek at the Plymouth Creek Trail. At the creek crossing, let your dog have a well-deserved wallow in one of the placid pools amid large boulders. Turn right (northeast) on the Plymouth Creek Trail and retrace your steps to the trailhead.

28. Meadowlark Trail Loop

Round trip: 2.25-mile loop
Hiking time: 2 hours
High point: 6450 feet
Elevation gain: 500 feet
Best hiking time: April–May; September–October
Maps: USGS Indian Hills; Trails Illustrated Boulder, Golden (no. 100); Jefferson County Open Space trails brochure
For more information: Jefferson County Open Space, (303) 271-5925

Getting there: From Colorado 470, exit at Wadsworth Avenue south-bound. Continue about 3 miles to South Deer Creek Canyon Road (almost directly across from entrance to Chatfield State Park). Turn right (west) and continue for 6.2 miles to Grizzly Drive on your left. Turn onto Grizzly Drive and continue 0.25 mile to the parking lot.

The Meadowlark Trail passes through one of Deer Creek Canyon Park's most interesting environments—the large groves of Gamble (scrub) oak, which are not that common in the foothills. Although small in stature, the scrub oak (*Quercus gambelli*) provides food and shelter for

Meadowlark Trail wanders through scrub vegetation.

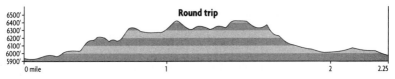

wildlife, including songbirds such as the meadowlark. The scrub oak turns a burnished orange in the fall, which adds visual pleasure to the hike.

The Meadowlark Trail is for hikers only, so if you are hiking on a weekend when there is heavy trail use by bicyclists, this trail will take you and your pet away from the traffic. There are pleasant picnic shelters near the trailhead, so you may like to lunch here after this short hike through meadows and groves of scrub oak.

Start on the Plymouth Creek Trail as it heads southwest. The trail ascends through sandy, dry meadow with intermittent scrub oak stands before dropping to Plymouth Creek where it crosses the creek on a bridge. Large boulders form shallow pools of water where your dog can get a drink and wet his paws.

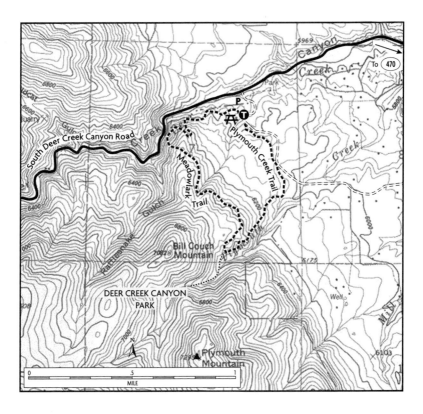

Plymouth Mountain (Hike 27) is ahead and the Meadowlark Trail bears off to the right (north). Follow the Meadowlark Trail up some rocky terrain, ascending switchbacks into the dense forest of ponderosa pine. At the top of the incline, look for a view of Deer Creek Canyon. Traverse the hillside through scrub oak and meadows and descend southeast to the trailhead.

29. High Line Canal: Waterton Canyon

Round trip: 5 miles
Hiking time: 3 hours
High point: 5560 feet
Elevation gain: Negligible
Best hiking time: April–October
Maps: Denver metro street map; High Line Canal booklet by Denver Water Board
For more information: Chatfield State Park, (303) 791-7275

Getting there: From Colorado 470 take the Wadsworth Avenue (Colorado Highway 121) exit southbound and continue on South Wadsworth Avenue for 4.8 miles to a clearly marked turnoff for Waterton Canyon. Turn left (east) onto Waterton Road and continue for 0.9 mile, past the trailhead and parking lot for the Colorado Trail and across a bridge over the South Platte River. Look for a large rock outcropping on your right. Park on the wide shoulder of the road. Entrance to the High Line Canal Trail is across the road. In the summer, the sign may be obscured by tall grass. There is a dirt parking lot a few hundred feet down the road on the left, whose entrance can also be obscured by grass in summer.

This hike lends itself to a shuttle. If you have two cars, continue on Waterton Road to where it ends at Rampart Range Road (County Road 5). Turn left (east) and drive for 1.2 miles to pullouts on either side of the road at a small bridge over the High Line Canal. There is a yellow

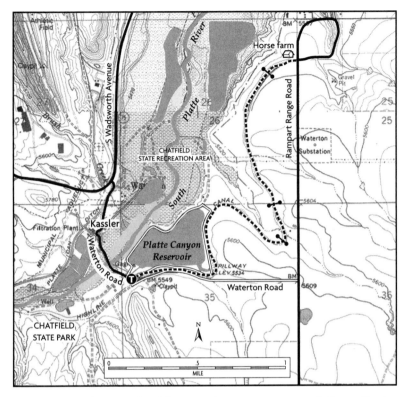

sign warning about a school bus stop just as you approach the pullouts. Leave one of the cars here and return in the second car to the High Line Canal access near the South Platte River.

The High Line Canal Trail in this area is open sunrise to sunset. Dogs must be on leash, and watch out for free-roaming cattle alongside the canal.

If you are looking for solitude, great views of Denver in the hazy distance, and a surprisingly realistic glimpse of what this area looked like around 1900, you will enjoy this casual, easy hike. The canal begins nearly 2 miles east of Waterton Canyon. A diversion dam on the South Platte River funnels water into a 600-foot-long tunnel. Water is siphoned beneath the river and carried in several flumes into the canal.

The canal traverses the southeast corner of Chatfield State Park, which oversees this portion of the canal trail. The canal and the adjacent right-of-way trail (and canal maintenance road) also pass through a private ranch where there is an original, tin-roofed homesteader's log cabin that is still in use. Since the ranch owns land on both sides of the canal, you may encounter cattle on the canal trail or see animals in the pasture along the canal. Make sure to keep your dog near you. This stretch of prairie is a surviving fragment of the tall-grass prairie pioneers tamed in the 1880s.

To begin hiking, cross Waterton Road to the canal trail and a large High Line Canal sign. Follow the trail as it contours around Platte Canyon Reservoir. A high chain-link fence surrounds the reservoir. The two white clapboard buildings are pumping sheds. Stop at the second shed to read a sign from a gentler age that advises, "Commit no nuisance here. These waters are public water supply. The defilement of these waters in any way is strictly not allowed."

Pass the canal's mile 2 marker on your left and continue to the first wire gate across the trail. Use the side wooden gate to continue. The canal sweeps in a large lazy loop creating a low pasture that is fed by Little Willow Creek. The trail is shaded by giant cottonwoods that were planted when the canal was built in the 1880s as an irrigation ditch for farms out in the prairie. These old, gnarled trees offer pleasant shade even on a hot day.

The bank leading down to the canal is low in places, so your dog can enjoy getting his paws wet. Keep a close watch on your pet. A herd of cattle may be grazing on the edge of the canal or resting in the shade of the cottonwoods. Pass a homesteader's log cabin on the opposite bank of the canal, then continue to the second wire gate and pass through the small wooden gate on the right.

Proceed to a third gate just short of Rampart Range Road. A horse farm is on the left. At the canal crossing over the road, turn around and return the way you came, or return to your starting trailhead in the car that you left as a car shuttle.

Meadows near Platte Canyon Reservoir are filled with wildflowers.

COLORADO SPRINGS

30. Waldo Canyon Loop

Round trip: 7.2-mile loop
Hiking time: 6 hours
High point: 8000 feet
Elevation gain: 1200 feet
Best hiking time: April–October
Maps: USGS Cascade; Trails Illustrated Pikes Peak, Canon City (no. 137)
For more information: Pike National Forest, Pikes Peak Ranger District, (719) 636-1602

Getting there: From the Interstate 25 intersection with Colorado Highway 21, take U.S. Highway 24 west 7.6 miles to the trailhead on the north side of the road. The trailhead is 2.2 miles west of Manitou Springs, and there is a parking area alongside the highway. A wooden sign and a post-and-rail fence mark the beginning of the trail. Arrive early, since on weekends the good-sized parking area fills quickly.

Certain hiking areas draw dog owners and their pets. In Denver, it's the Cherry Creek State Park off-leash area and the urban Washington Park. In the Denver foothills, it's Deer Creek Canyon. And in Colorado Springs it's Waldo Canyon. Waldo Canyon is easy to reach and easy to hike, because

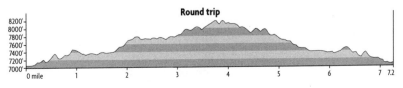

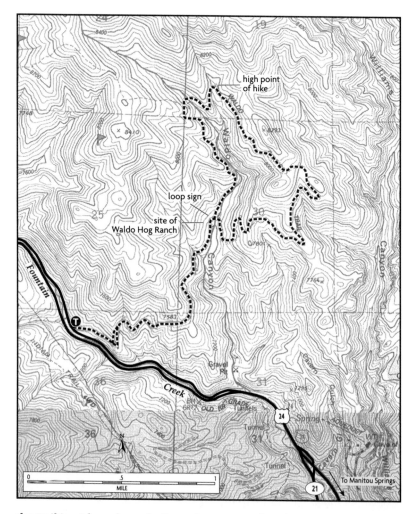

the trail is wide and easy both on dog paws and on human eyes. The canyon is famous for its beautiful wildflowers, best May through August. And the trip is educational, too. Signs along the route describe the canyon's unique geologic features. For these reasons, this is one of the most heavily used trails in the Pikes Peak district, so the best time to go is early and on weekdays, to avoid crowds and mountain bikers. Nonetheless, the trip is worth it even at busy times. Your dog must be leashed on this hike.

From the trailhead, start out on a set of timber-hewn steps, which will quickly lead you into a quiet mountain environment of rocky spires, wildflowers, and stands of evergreen forest.

On the trail, a sign identifies the pink-colored rock as Pikes Peak granite, about 1 billion years old. This is the predominant rock along the canyon. The pink color sets off scrub oak and mountain mahogany growing along the trail. Early in the season blue penstemon grows abundantly in the canyon. The trail continues through a pine and fir forest.

The trail drops into several ravines, then crosses a ridge to access the canyon after about 1 mile from the trailhead. The trail descends into the canyon and enters a meadow, fed by a creek which flows through the canyon and offers enticing opportunities for your dog to get refreshed at the half dozen or so shallow crossings of the at-times-sluggish stream.

The meadow is thought to be the site of the Waldo Hog Ranch for which the canyon is named. At 1.6 miles there is a sign that marks the beginning of the loop of the canyon. It says "Waldo Canyon Loop 3.5 miles." You can go either way, although this hike turns (right) to do the loop counterclockwise. Spectacular views of Pikes Peak are just ahead. The trail begins to climb in earnest along a switchback which reveal the flanks and distant summit of Pikes Peak, made famous during the nineteenth-century gold rush when Conestoga wagons bore signs saying, "Pikes Peak or Bust."

Reach the high point of the hike at 3.5 miles from the trailhead. The rest of the hike is downhill, so enjoy the scenery and dawdle with your dog at the stream crossings.

As you hike through the woods you may spot deer or bighorn sheep,

Waldo Canyon has meadows famous for abundant wildflowers such as the sego lily in early spring.

or your dog may pick up their scent. Make sure that your dog is under control to prevent wildlife harassment.

As the trail flattens out, a sign points out a geological oddity in the canyon's rocks—a major break in the geologic record. Here, Cambrian Sawatch sandstone overlies the Pikes Peak granite, with about 500 million years of rock deposits missing between the two segments. A large outcrop later on illustrates the nonconformity of rock deposits.

Toward the end of the loop, vistas open to the south and afford a view of Colorado Springs and Broadmoor, the famous resort. The trail next enters a ponderosa pine forest and the trail descends along the stream, whose banks bloom profusely with wildflowers. The pretty, delicate red flowers are shooting stars.

Meet up with the beginning of the loop portion and turn right to retrace your steps to the trailhead.

31. The Crags

Round trip: 4 miles
Hiking time: 2.5 hours
High point: 10,728 feet
Elevation gain: 800 feet
Best hiking time: May–October
Maps: USGS Cascade; Trails Illustrated Pikes Peak, Canon City (no. 137)
For more information: Pike National Forest, Pikes Peak Ranger District, (719) 636-1602

Getting there: From Colorado Springs, take U.S. Highway 24 west to Woodland Park and continue on to Divide. Turn south on Colorado Highway 67. Drive 4 miles and turn left on Forest Road 383. Continue for 2.5 miles to the Crags Campground and trailhead. Parking is available at the east end of the campground, next to the trailhead.

This trail leads to the Crags, a group of rock pinnacle formations. The trail is restricted to hikers and horsemen, so it is not as busy as others in the area on weekends. The hike is on the northwest flank of Pikes Peak. If you think that someday you may want to hike this Fourteener, a trip to the Crags will give you a feel for the mountain.

For most of the way, the trail is covered with decomposing needles from the evergreens. The ground is moist and is easy on your dog's paws. A stream is near the campground but there is no reliable source of water on the hike, so make sure to take some along. Your dog must be on a leash.

A scant 0.1 mile from the trailhead, you will come to a fork. Stay left and continue along the trail marked "664" (the right fork, marked "664A" ascends Pikes Peak). The trail continues on a gradual incline through pine

Sandstone outcroppings along the trail

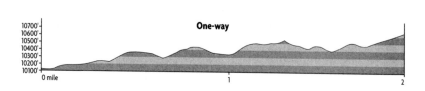

forest. The forest is interspersed with tall rock outcrops that create striking images, sometimes not unlike the famous rock formations in the Garden of the Gods in Colorado Springs.

The climb is gradual for the first mile as the trail emerges from the trees into a sunny meadow covered with wildflowers and rimmed by evergreens. Next, the trail veers left up the valley. At a second fork bear right and head for an aspen forest. Here the trail becomes increasingly steep as you trudge up the final pitch toward an overlook. Once out in the open, the trail is marked with rock cairns to the overlook and the Crags. By then, you are near the summit. Scramble up the rocks to the flat top and take in the 360-degree vista before returning to the trailhead.

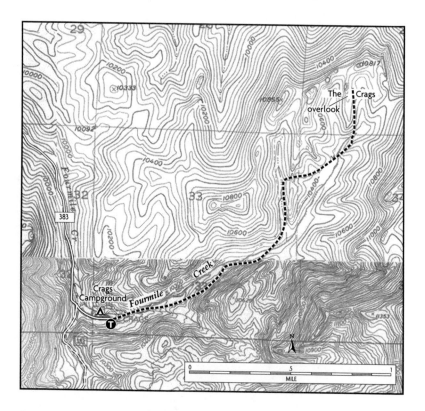

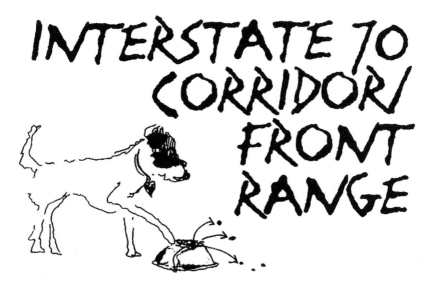

INTERSTATE 70 CORRIDOR/ FRONT RANGE

32. Silver Dollar and Murray Lakes

Round trip: 4.4 miles
Hiking time: 3 hours
High point: 12,400 feet
Elevation gain: 800 feet
Best hiking time: Late May–September
Maps: USGS Mount Evans; USGS Montezuma; Trails Illustrated Idaho Springs, Georgetown, Loveland Pass (no. 104)
For more information: Arapaho National Forest, Clear Creek Ranger District, (303) 567-3000

Getting there: From Denver, drive west on Interstate 70 to exit 228/ Georgetown. Leave the highway and drive under the interstate overpass to the stop sign. Turn right and follows signs for Guanella Pass through Georgetown. At 9 miles and on the first dirt road intersection

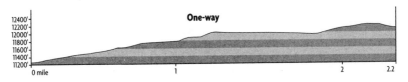

after Guanella Pass Campground, look for a wooden sign that says "Silver Dollar Lake" with an arrow pointing to the right. The trailhead is down this dirt road 0.75 mile ahead. At this point, if you do not have a four-wheel-drive vehicle, you may want to park your car, although a passenger car driven with extra caution can make it to the small parking lot at the trailhead.

Silver Dollar Lake Trail is famous for its wildflowers: botanists report that 100 species bloom along the trail. The trail traverses the south side of the narrow valley. The large lake at the bottom of the gulch is Naylor Lake and is privately owned. At the head of the valley, Silver Dollar and Murray Lakes are stocked and trout anglers can often be seen along the shoreline.

Begin hiking at the west end of the parking lot. The trail curves moderately steeply through a thinning forest and crosses a small creek your dog may enjoy exploring while you admire the blue monkshood and larkspur wildflowers growing in abundance in the dappled shade. Soon the trail reaches timberline as it contours along the north flank of Square Top Mountain that rises steeply to the left. Slightly ahead and also to the left beyond Square Top's slope is Argentine Peak.

The trail is narrow but fairly easy, with one short section that is a bit difficult—the trail drops into a shallow ravine and crosses a stubborn snowfield that sometimes lasts all summer. Use caution here. Once past this dip, the trail levels off as it passes through soft, boggy terrain and thick willows. The willows recede at Silver Dollar Lake (1.6 miles from

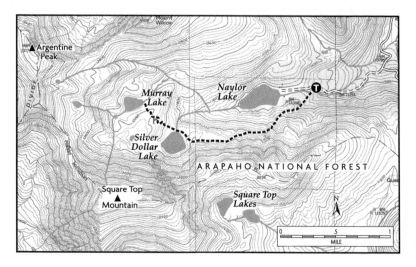

Willows crowd the trail to Silver Dollar Lake.

the trailhead) and both the lake and the outlet stream will provide your dog with some delightful refreshment. Here marsh marigolds and the showy red Parry's primrose bloom in abundance.

After lunch and a rest, you can turn around here or scramble to Murray Lake, 0.6 mile above and to the right (north) of Silver Dollar Lake.

33. Mount Wilcox and Otter Mountain

Round trip: 6.8-mile loop
Hiking time: 8 hours
High point: 13,608 feet
Elevation gain: 2600 feet
Best hiking time: Late June–early September
Maps: USGS Mount Evans; USGS Montezuma; Trails Illustrated Idaho Springs, Georgetown, Loveland Pass (no. 104)
For more information: Arapaho National Forest, Clear Creek Ranger District, (303) 567-3000

Getting there: From Denver, drive west on Interstate 70 to exit 228/Georgetown. Leave the highway and drive under the interstate overpass

The ridge to Mount Wilcox and Otter Mountain

to the stop sign. Turn right and follows signs for Guanella Pass through Georgetown. At 9 miles and on the first dirt road intersection after Guanella Pass Campground, look for a wooden sign that says "Silver Dollar Lake" with an arrow pointing to the right. The trailhead is down this dirt road 0.75 mile ahead. At this point, if you do not have a four-wheel-drive vehicle, you may want to park your car, although a passenger car driven with extra caution can make it to the small parking lot at the trailhead.

Silver Dollar Lake Trail is famous for its wildflowers but it is also the gateway to a satisfying loop trip above timberline that skirts Square Top Mountain's north face and climbs a Thirteener and a 12,000-foot peak. Only attempt this hike early in the day and in good weather. There is no easy way to seek shelter from a thunderstorm once you are past Silver Dollar and Murray Lakes.

Most maps do not show a trail to Mount Wilcox and Otter Mountain, although the loop hike is regularly featured in trip schedules of the Colorado Mountain Club. Still, you will need your topographic map—it will prove useful on the way down from Otter Mountain even though your canine companion will probably be leading the way.

Begin hiking on the Silver Dollar Lake Trail (Hike 32) at the west end of the parking lot. The trail curves moderately steeply through a thinning forest and crosses a small creek your dog may find enjoyable. Continue up loose switchbacks to timberline, then traverse the south side of the narrow valley that contains three lakes. The first and largest is Naylor Lake, which is privately owned. The second is Silver Dollar Lake at the base of Square Top. The third and smallest is Murray Lake, tucked away on a shelf at the head of the valley.

Silver Dollar Lake is a good break stop. The flat, sandy shoreline and the numerous rivulets flowing out of the lake are the kind of water and soft terrain dogs love to explore. If there are no fishermen angling for trout, throw a ball or a stick into the calm lake and enjoy a game of fetch with your dog.

After the rest, the hard work begins. But before you proceed, check the weather. You should be at Silver Dollar Lake no later than 10:00 AM If the weather looks fine, scramble up to Murray Lake on a well-defined trail. The lake offers the last opportunity for your dog to take a swim, although rivulets and streamlets flowing into the lake from the slope continue to provide water and refreshment for your dog as you tackle Mount Wilcox.

From the east side of Murray Lake pick up the faint trail that is occasionally marked with rock cairns and head due north to reach the ridge. Turn east on the ridge and ascend Mount Wilcox. The terrain is tundra

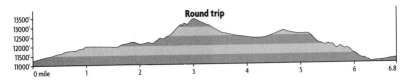

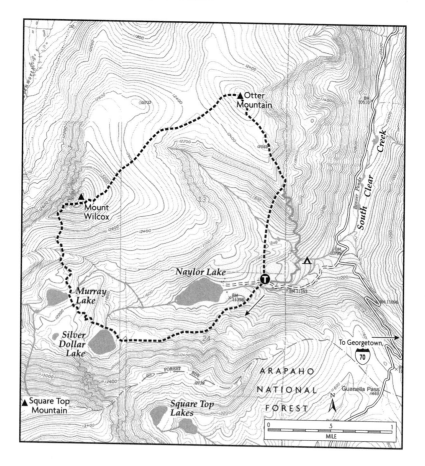

with few rocks except close to the summit. Your dog should have no problem on this terrain since the ridge is wide and mostly soft tundra.

After checking for clear skies at the summit of Mount Wilcox, continue along the ridge in a northeasterly direction, dropping 300 feet into the saddle between Mount Wilcox and Otter Mountain.

Ascend the tundra slope of Otter Mountain. Once on the summit look nearly due south to locate a high point, 12,560 feet on the topo map. This is your next destination. After that point, the route descends more rapidly toward timberline on a steep slope. You will now be headed due south. There are few faint trails in this area and you will be bushwhacking. If you catch sight of Naylor Lake, head toward its eastern end. Keep an eye on your dog in the forest, since at times the slope is quite steep.

Continue descending until the grade levels off. At this point you should intersect the access road to the trailhead. If your descent was too easterly, you will enter the Guanella Pass Campground that you passed before turning onto the access road. If this happens, you will need to hike up the road to your parked car.

34. Rosalie Trail

One-way: 12.4 miles
Hiking time: 9–10 hours or backpack
High point: 11,800 feet
Elevation gain: 1100 feet
Best hiking time: July–September
Maps: USGS Mount Evans; USGS Harris Park; Trails Illustrated Idaho Springs, Georgetown, Loveland Pass (no. 104)
For more information: Pike National Forest, South Platte Ranger District, (303) 275-5610; Arapaho National Forest, Clear Creek Ranger District, (303) 567-3000

Getting there: Rosalie Trail has two trailheads. To get to the northern trailhead, take Interstate 70 to exit 228/Georgetown. Go under the I-70 overpass to the stop sign and turn right. Follow the signs for the Guanella Pass Scenic and Historic Byway for 11 miles to Guanella Pass (11,669 feet). The road is paved to the Excel hydroelectric plant and then turns to gravel. Once you reach the pass, park in the large parking lot on your left. The Rosalie Trail trailhead is at the southeast corner of the parking lot.

To reach the southeastern trailhead at Deer Creek, drive west from Denver on U.S. Highway 285 approximately 28 miles to the traffic light before the top of Crow Hill. Turn right (northwest) onto County Road 43 and drive in a northwesterly direction for 6.8 miles to a fork in the road. Bear left and drive 2.1 miles, staying right at the Deer Creek Campground, to the trailhead parking area.

After leaving one car at Deer Creek, return to US 285 and turn right

Round trip

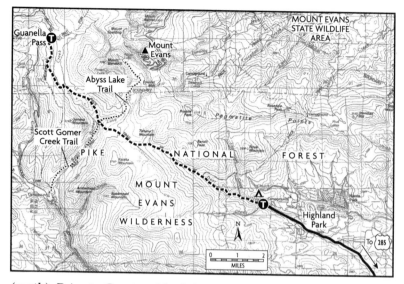

(south). Drive to Grant and look for the Guanella Pass Scenic and Historic Byway sign on your right. Turn right and continue to the pass and the northern trailhead.

This is a long and rugged trail that crosses the Mount Evans Wilderness from Guanella Pass in Arapaho National Forest southeast to Deer Creek, near US 285, in the Pike National Forest. Rosalie Trail offers excellent opportunities for a 2- to 3-day backpack, although it can be traversed one-way in a long and arduous day. It lends itself to a shuttle with one car at Guanella Pass and the other at Deer Creek. Starting at Guanella Pass entails less of an elevation gain, since some sections are decidedly downhill. Hiking from Deer Creek is harder, but the vistas are better.

The Rosalie Trail offers a variety of terrain and scenery. The trail is mostly through a dense and lush Colorado forest that is watered by numerous creeks your dog will enjoy. Views are spectacular and include the southwestern slope of Mount Bierstadt and the glacial cirque on the south side of Mount Evans. The trail snakes along the base of Mount Bierstadt and Mount Evans, two of the four Fourteeners in the Front Range. Several stretches of the trail are above timberline. The Guanella Pass area is notorious for sudden, intense afternoon thunderstorms, hence the lushness of the forest. This weather pattern also affects hikers, particularly when they are hiking above timberline. Because the trail is almost entirely in designated wilderness, wilderness regulations apply and your dog must remain on a leash.

From Guanella Pass, take the trail leading south out of the parking area. Pass the willow bog on the left and climb a hill as the trail veers east and south to contours around the hill. Farther south, the trail climbs the ridge, then gradually descends southeast into willows where a marker post shows the way.

Once past the willows, the trail enters the aspen and lodgepole pine forest. Shortly after reaching the trees, the trail intersects the Scott Gomer Creek and Abyss Lake Trails at 4.5 miles. Then it continues into the Three Mile Creek drainage to cross Three Mile Creek Trail at a large and pleasant meadow. This meadow is at just over 6 miles, the halfway point from Guanella Pass to Deer Creek.

From here, switchbacks take you up Rosalie Pass, a good place for a rest to admire the vistas of Mount Bierstadt and the sheer south flank of Mount Evans.

Then it's downhill. The trail descends into the Deer Creek drainage, with more opportunities for your dog to frolic in water. Near the wilderness boundary, the trail joins an old logging road to an intersection with the Tanglewood Trail. On its final stretch, the Rosalie Trail turns south and goes downstream to the Deer Creek trailhead.

Backpacking: If you plan a round-trip backpack, it may be better to start at Deer Creek and get the significant elevation gain out of the way early on in the outing. Numerous meadows, large and small, offer a variety of camping opportunities.

Start of the Rosalie Trail on Guanella Pass

35. Square Top Lakes

Round trip: 4.2 miles
Hiking time: 3 hours
High point: 12,300 feet
Elevation gain: 600 feet
Best hiking time: June–September
Maps: USGS Mount Evans; Trails Illustrated Idaho Springs, Georgetown, Loveland Pass (no. 104)
For more information: Arapaho National Forest, Clear Creek Ranger District, (303) 567-3000

Getting there: Take Interstate 70 to exit 228/Georgetown. Go under the I-70 overpass to the stop sign and turn right. Follow the signs for the Guanella Pass Scenic and Historic Byway for 11 miles to Guanella Pass (11,669 feet). The road is paved to the Excel hydroelectric plant and then turns to gravel. Once you reach the pass, park in the large parking lot on your left. The Square Top Mountain trail is across the road (on the west side of the pass).

Pink Indian paintbrush blooms profusely along the trail to Square Top lakes.

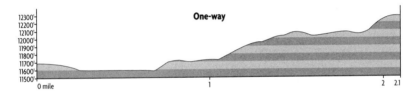

Square Top Mountain (Hike 36) sits to the west of Guanella Pass. It missed being a Fourteener by 206 feet and so does not attract the crowds streaming up Mount Bierstadt on the east side of the pass. The trail leads to alpine lakes as it follows an unused rutted road through a boggy area with little rivulets your dog will enjoy.

Begin hiking west on flat terrain, then drop gently into the boggy area, where such wildflowers as little pink elephants, queen's crown, and king's crown bloom profusely in late July. From the bog, the trail rises gradually to thick willows and the first of two lakes at 2 miles. Here, carpets of rosy and yellow paintbrush grow near the willows.

The second lake is about 0.1 mile farther on. The willows give way to

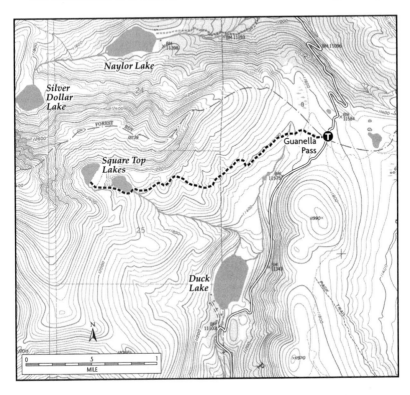

grasses and boulders at the lakeshore and your pet can enjoy a refreshing dip. Hike 36 continues to Square Top Mountain.

Return the way you came, admiring Mount Bierstadt and the sawtooth ridge that connects it to giant Mount Evans.

36. Square Top Mountain

Round trip: 6.2 miles
Hiking time: 5–6 hours
High point: 13,794 feet
Elevation gain: 2120 feet
Best hiking time: Late June–September
Maps: USGS Mount Evans; USGS Montezuma; Trails Illustrated Idaho Springs, Georgetown, Loveland Pass (no. 104)
For more information: Arapaho National Forest, Clear Creek Ranger District, (303) 567-3000

Getting there: Take Interstate 70 to exit 228/Georgetown. Go under the I-70 overpass to the stop sign and turn right. Follow the signs for the Guanella Pass Scenic and Historic Byway for 11 miles to Guanella Pass, 11,669 feet. The road is paved to the Excel hydroelectric plant and then turns to gravel. Once you reach the pass, park in the large parking lot on your left. The Square Top Mountain Trail is across the road (on the west side of the pass).

Square Top Mountain, the big mountain to the west at Guanella Pass, missed being a Fourteener by a mere 206 feet. It is a pleasant and comfortable ascent, first on a flat old wagon road, then on a narrowing trail, and finally following rock cairns across a mostly grassy tundra. If you are worried about the hardiness of your dog's paws but still want his companionship while climbing a tall peak, this may be the climb.

The entire hike is above timberline and you need to watch the weather carefully. Storms in this area are famous for their sudden appearance and their severity.

One-way

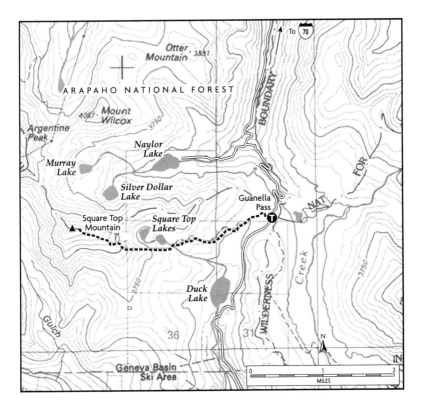

Hike west from the pass on soft, often marshy ground that is covered with wildflowers, following an old rutted road that still shows two tracks here and there. The road dips slightly but then begins its unrelenting ascent and narrows into a well-defined trail.

At 2 miles, pass Square Top Lakes (Hike 35) to the right (north), which are nestled in thick willows. You will also cross a creek in this area, so your pet can be refreshed and hydrated. Watch your pet for excessive panting or sluggishness, both indicators of altitude problems.

Continue on a steeper grade up the ridge past two ridge bumps. At about 13,700 feet the trail levels off into a long summit plateau. This wide gentle ridge extends west to a high point where there is a small summit cairn and a sign-in register. The 360-degree view offers the Tenmile and Mosquito Ranges to the west and south. To the east rise Mount Evans and Mount Bierstadt. Grays Peak and Torreys Peak, two more Fourteeners, are to the northwest.

Return the way you came.

Square Top Mountain rises west of Guanella Pass. (Photo by Stefan Krusze)

37. Grizzly Gulch

Round trip: 4 miles
Hiking time: 2 hours
High point: 11,300 feet
Elevation gain: 900 feet
Best hiking time: May–October
Maps: USGS Grays Peak; Trails Illustrated Idaho Springs, Georgetown, Loveland Pass (no. 104)
For more information: Arapaho National Forest, Clear Creek Ranger District, (303) 567-3000

Getting there: Take Interstate 70 to exit 221/Bakerville. Follow the Stevens Gulch Road south for 1.5 miles. Turn right onto the dirt road that goes up Grizzly Gulch. There are plenty of parking spaces on both sides of the road.

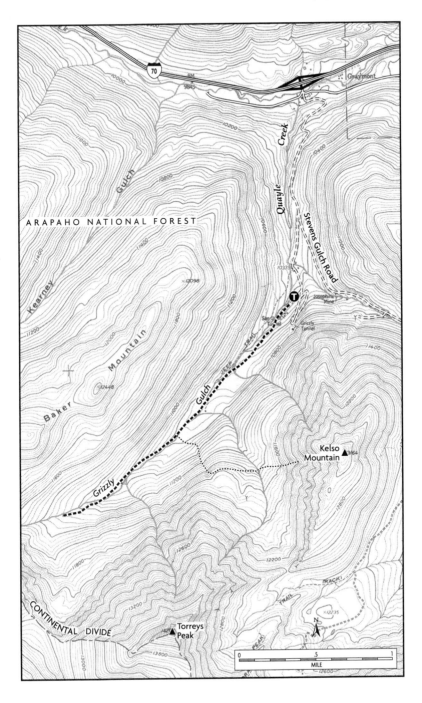

Grizzly Gulch rises through a conifer forest.

If you are wondering why so many cars are heading up Stevens Gulch, the answer is that it is the primary access for climbing Grays Peak and Torreys Peak, two very popular Fourteeners. Grizzly Gulch provides access to Kelso Mountain and Grizzly Peak, which are Thirteeners. Don't be surprised if you meet no one on this short, pleasant hike.

The working and abandoned mines along Grizzly Gulch are a present-day reminder of Colorado's early history. In 1859, John H. Gregory was the first to strike lode gold in the mountains. Soon, Clear Creek County became one of the richest areas in the world and such towns as Central City, Black Hawk, and Empire sprang up.

Today, the depleted and abandoned mines dot the landscape, sometimes reaching as high as the Continental Divide as in the case of mines in Grizzly Gulch. As you hike, observe the discolored piles of tailings, rusted derricks, and machinery on the flanks of Kelso and Grizzly Peak. In this gulch, the most famous mine is the Josephine Mine on the left, at the head of the gulch where the hike begins.

In addition, several vacation homes are on the right, a short distance into the gulch. But once past them, the hike takes you into a beautiful pine forest with lovely vistas as you gain elevation. Since the hike is along the old, but maintained road, it is accessible up until the first snowfall.

Your dog will enjoy this hike, too. The stream offers numerous access points for frolicking and hydration. The trail is wide and relatively rock-free at the start, and once you are in the trees, the ground is soft and spongy, a benefit for dogs with tender paws.

Hike up the gulch for 2 miles or until you wish to turn around. A trail bears off to the left to ascend Kelso on a tricky talus field. Grizzly Peak is ahead and is occasionally climbed from this side, but mostly it is reached from Loveland Pass.

Return the way you came.

38. Herman Lake

Round trip: 5.6 miles
Hiking time: 5 hours
High point: 12,000 feet
Elevation gain: 1700 feet
Best hiking time: July–August
Maps: USGS Grays Peak; USGS Loveland Pass; Trails Illustrated
  Idaho Springs, Georgetown, Loveland Pass (no. 104)
For more information: Arapaho National Forest, Clear Creek Ranger
  District, (303) 567-3000

Getting there: From Denver take Interstate 70 west for 50 miles to exit 218, the last exit before U.S. Highway 6 and the Eisenhower Tunnel. Turn right at the bottom of the off-ramp. Proceed on a dirt road for a short distance to a large gravel parking lot with new and well-maintained restroom facilities.

Dogs love this hike because of the numerous rivulets and minor streamlet crossings along the trail. This is an enormously popular trail, so the Forest Service now requires that dogs be leashed. However, this should not deter you from taking your dog on this hike. Once up the old lumber road, the trail intersects numerous rivulets that flow down the slope into Herman Creek. In the lodgepole pine forest, the ground is spongy and pleasant to hike on. When you get to Herman Lake, dogs know exactly what to do. Most hikers let them off leash for a quick swim or a game of "fetch" in the still but frigid water of the alpine tarn.

Sign in at the register, then proceed on a narrow trail for a short distance to a Forest Service sign indicating Herman Lake to the left and Watrous

Gulch (Hike 40) to the right. Turn left for the lake onto an old sawmill road that is gravelly and climbs rather steeply along a creek on your left.

Pass through groves of aspen and emerge from the deciduous trees after a mile into a series of alpine meadows separated by stands of conifers and willows in the moist areas. Subalpine flowers, especially blue columbine (the Colorado state flower), bloom profusely in July in this area.

The ground in the meadows is often swampy and soft, so your dog should not develop sore paws. And once you are in the meadows, the stream banks level off and provide easy access for a quick dip.

Despite the many creek crossings and wet spots, Herman Creek veers away from the trail but is still within a short distance. After the meadows and moderately rising trail, often over logs in the wettest spots, the

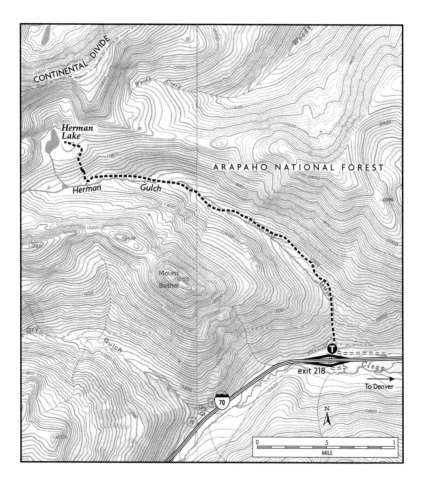

Trail rises upvalley to Herman Lake. (Photo by Stefan Krusze)

trail begins to climb again and you encounter rocky terrain with gravelly ground and numerous switchbacks.

The switchbacks end on a shelf that holds Herman Lake, below the majestic ridge of the Continental Divide. Once on the flat shelf, the trail swings left and is well marked with rock cairns that lead the way through willows and cinquefoil shrubs. In wet spots look for the scarlet Parry's primrose and marsh marigolds.

Herman Lake is truly a paradise for dogs, especially retrievers who love plunging into the icy waters to retrieve a hurled ball or stick. The lake is above timberline so watch the weather. Hike 39 continues to Pettingell Peak.

Return the way you came.

39. Pettingell Peak

Round trip: 8 miles
Hiking time: 8–9 hours
High point: 13,553 feet
Elevation gain: 3053 feet
Best hiking time: July–August
Maps: USGS Grays Peak; USGS Loveland Pass; Trails Illustrated Idaho Springs, Georgetown, Loveland Pass (no. 104)
For more information: Arapaho National Forest, Clear Creek Ranger District, (303) 567-3000

Getting there: From Denver take Interstate 70 west for 50 miles to exit 218, the last exit before U.S. Highway 6 and the Eisenhower Tunnel.

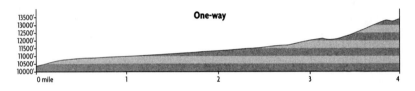

Turn right at the bottom of the off-ramp. Proceed on a dirt road for a short distance to a large gravel parking lot with new and well-maintained restroom facilities.

Pettingell Peak is the highest peak in the Clear Creek group north of Loveland Pass and forms part of the Continental Divide. The climb is steep but for the most part on grass tundra. A talus field is near the ridge and a moderate boulder scramble takes you to the summit. Both you and your pet should be in fine physical shape before attempting Pettingell.

Begin hiking at 10,320 feet from the Herman Gulch parking lot. Hike a narrow trail for a short distance to a Forest Service sign indicating Herman Lake (Hike 38) to the left and Watrous Gulch (Hike 40) to the right. Turn left onto an old sawmill road that is gravelly and climbs rather steeply along Herman Creek on your left. This first portion of the hike is up a high valley, through aspen and conifer forests and through meadows that in winter become avalanche chutes.

Leave the creek and bear northwest on the trail and up several sharp gravelly switchbacks to reach timberline and a shelf on which Herman Lake rests. Turn left and proceed to the lake. The nearly 3-mile hike to the lake nets you about 1700 feet elevation gain, just over half of the gain on this hike. Pause at the lake for a snack and let your dog enjoy a dip.

The imposing crenellated mountain directly west of the lake is The Citadel (13,294 feet). It is a technical climb with a razor-sharp ridge and significant drop-offs. Pettingell Peak is farther along the northwest ridge of the Continental Divide. It is slightly to the northwest of the lake and its southeastern face is grassy.

You should think twice before climbing Pettingell if you or your dog are fatigued or you reached Herman Lake later than 10:00 AM Storms come up suddenly in this area and generally occur in the afternoon. You will be above timberline the entire time and the climb is steep.

Opposite: Pettingell Peak from Herman Gulch

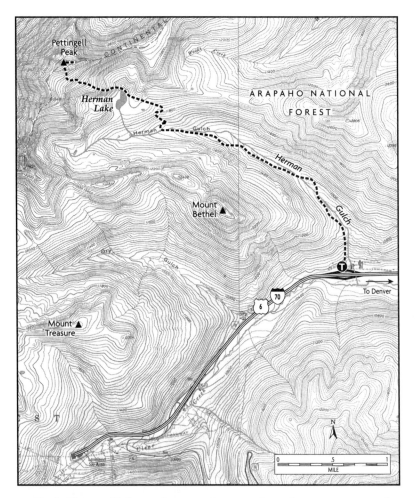

Circle Herman Lake to the east, then north, and contour across the spongy, grassy slope in a westerly direction following a trail that occasionally disappears into snowdrifts that last into the summer. Aim at the southwest ridge of Pettingell, whose summit is clearly visible to the northwest. Follow a faint trail across a scree slope to reach a low point on the ridge. Turn right (north) on the ridge and scramble over boulders to the summit, marked by a large cairn. Sign in at the register hidden in the rock pile.

The view to the north and east is panoramic, with Longs Peak on the horizon. To the west rise the jagged peaks of the Gore Range and to the southeast are three of the Front Range's Fourteeners—Mount Evans and Torreys and Grays Peaks.

Descend the way you came and follow the Herman Lake Trail back to your car.

40. Watrous Gulch

Round trip: 5 miles
Hiking time: 4 hours
High point: 11,900 feet
Elevation gain: 1500 feet
Best hiking time: May–September
Maps: USGS Grays Peak; USGS Loveland Pass; Trails Illustrated Idaho Springs, Georgetown, Loveland Pass (no. 104)
For more information: Arapaho National Forest, Clear Creek Ranger District, (303) 567-3000

Getting there: From Denver take Interstate 70 west for 50 miles to exit 218, the last exit before U.S. Highway 6 and the Eisenhower Tunnel. Turn right at the bottom of the off-ramp. Proceed on a dirt road for a short distance to a large gravel parking lot with new and well-maintained restroom facilities.

Watrous Gulch is also under leash restrictions, but it is far less popular than the Herman Lake Trail, although it has features that you and your dog will enjoy. After passing through a forest where there is significant fallen timber, the trail emerges at timberline at Watrous Creek. This is a shallow, wide and slow-moving stream that can be crossed easily by hopping from rock to rock. Your dog will enjoy the cool water and the opportunity to splash around. Beyond the creek, the trail turns north and ascends the gulch through luxuriant grasses and fields of wildflowers. The incline is moderate and there are numerous places where you can stop and let your pet roll in the grass.

Sign in at the register, then proceed on a narrow trail for a short distance to a Forest Service sign indicating Herman Lake (Hikes 38 and 39) to the left and Watrous Gulch to the right.

Turn right and follow the narrow trail, which has many rocks and winds upward among the trees in an easterly direction. The forest is filled with fallen timber and boulders, the result of a major flood in July 1999. This is a good place to keep your dog near you, since deviating from the trail can be hazardous because of the downed trees.

After a mile you will emerge from the forest and pass through an area of stumps, the result of clear-cutting in the nineteenth century during the height of the mining era. As you approach timberline, the trail levels off and crosses Watrous Creek on logs and rocks and turns north. Once you reach timberline and the creek, the tundra opens up and the trail widens. Here is a good place to take a break or play Frisbee or a ball game with your pet.

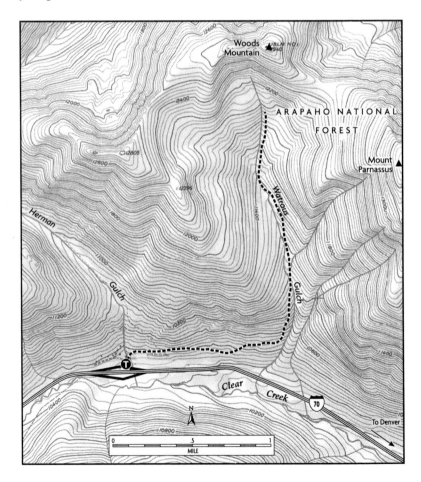

The trail skirts Mount Parnassus (13,524 feet), which rises to the east. Continue up the gulch, heading toward the saddle between Parnassus and Woods Mountain (12,940 feet), whose summit is dead ahead (and on the Hike 41 loop).

Watrous Gulch above timberline is famous for a profusion of wildflowers during the summer months. Find a level spot to sit down and admire the view. The cone-shaped peak to the south, on the other side of I-70, is Mount Sniktau (13,234 feet).

Return the way you came.

Forest Service sign at trail junction

41. Woods Mountain and Mount Machebeuf

Round trip: 6 miles
Hiking time: 7 hours
High point: 12,940 feet
Elevation gain: 2900 feet
Best hiking time: June–September
Maps: USGS Grays Peak; USGS Loveland Pass; Trails Illustrated Idaho Springs, Georgetown, Loveland Pass (no. 104)
For more information: Arapaho National Forest, Clear Creek Ranger District, (303) 567-3000

Getting there: From Denver take Interstate 70 west for 50 miles to exit 218, the last exit before U.S. Highway 6 and the Eisenhower Tunnel. Turn right at the bottom of the off-ramp. Proceed on a dirt road for a short distance to a large gravel parking lot with new and well-maintained restroom facilities.

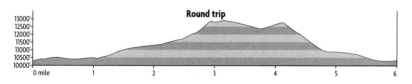

This hike offers solitude for you since most hikers favor the Herman Lake Trail (Hike 38) and also plenty of soft tundra to keep your dog's paws unchafed. Although steep and long, the hike takes you to a ridgetop that is seldom visited and that offers fantastic views. Unless you return the way you came, the second half of the hike takes you cross-country into a rapid descent down rock-free slopes and old avalanche chutes into Herman Gulch.

Sign in at the register, then proceed on a narrow trail for a short distance to a Forest Service sign indicating Herman Lake (Hikes 38 and 39) to the left and Watrous Gulch (Hike 40) to the right.

Turn right and follow the trail up Watrous Gulch. The trail rises through

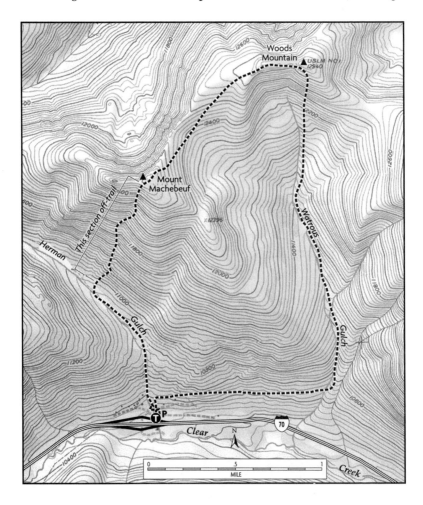

Woods Mountain from Herman Gulch

a forest filled with dead lumber and boulders, the result of a major flood in July 1999. Just short of timberline the trail levels off, passes a clear-cut from 100 years ago, then swings north. Woods Mountain (12,940 feet) is ahead.

Continue climbing out of the gulch and aim for the low point on the ridge, which is the saddle between Woods Mountain and Mount Parnassus (13,574 feet) to the east. The climb becomes steep but is on grassy tundra. The ridge is broad and curved and offers panoramic views in all directions. Once on the saddle, turn left (west) and continue to Woods' summit.

At this point you have a choice. You have climbed about 3 miles and 2000 feet. If you feel strong, proceed along the ridge to the clearly visible high point to the southwest. On many topo maps this point is identified as Point 12805, although it was named some years ago for Joseph Machebeuf, the first Catholic bishop of Denver.

Mount Machebeuf is 1 mile southwest of Woods Mountain. As you drop into the saddle between the two peaks, you lose about 400 feet, which you will have to climb again. The good news is that the trail is clearly marked and for the most part free of scree and boulders.

Once you have summited Machebeuf, you can return the way you came, or take a bearing on Mount Sniktau (13,234 feet), the cone-shaped mountain across the valley and the most prominent peak due south. Begin on this bearing, contouring down the southwestern slope of Machebeuf. There is no real trail here, and the slope is grassy and free of rocks but very steep. Try to stay away from the trees as you near timberline, and instead head for one of the many meadows on old avalanche chutes in Herman Gulch.

Eventually you will reach Herman Lake Trail. Turn left (east) and continue to the junction of the Herman Lake and Watrous Gulch Trails. Turn right and back to the parking lot.

42. Mount Sniktau

Round trip: 3 miles
Hiking time: 2–3 hours
High point: 13,234 feet
Elevation gain: 1224 feet
Best hiking time: Late July–August
Maps: USGS Loveland Pass; Trails Illustrated Idaho Springs, Georgetown, Loveland Pass (no. 104)
For more information: Arapaho National Forest, Clear Creek Ranger District, (303) 567-3000

Getting there: Take Interstate 70 from Denver west and exit onto U.S. Highway 6, the last exit before the Eisenhower Tunnel. Take US 6 to Loveland Pass and park on the left in the parking lot adjacent to the large sign describing the Continental Divide.

Many hikers wonder where Mount Sniktau got its name. The origin is not Native American, as some think. Sniktau was the pen name of E. H. N. Patterson, who worked as a journalist in Clear Creek County in the 1860s. Patterson is best known for his friendship with Edgar Allan Poe. The Poe archives in Baltimore contain a letter, written June 7, 1849, that identifies Patterson as the publisher of the *Oquawka Spectator* in Oquawka, Illinois. In the letter Patterson discusses his proposed publication of Poe's projected literary periodical, *The Stylus*.

Aside from this bit of literary lore, why hike Mount Sniktau? It is a short hike for anyone that wants a true alpine experience. It will tax your and your pet's stamina at high altitude and in adverse conditions. Do this hike before attempting a Fourteener with or without your pet. The wind can roar, weather can roll in suddenly, but there are no sharp drop-offs and the hike is essentially a ridge walk with fantastic views in every direction. Some hikers say that on a clear day looking north you can see Wyoming.

Start the hike no later than 9:00 AM, since the entire hike is above tim-

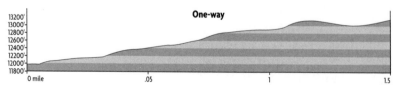

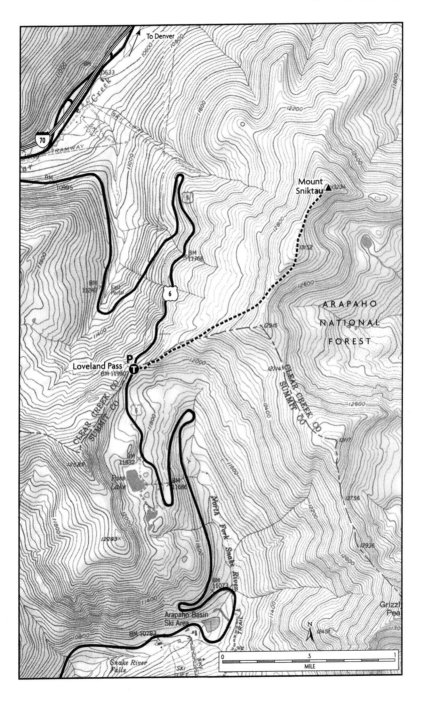

berline and the chance of violent thunderstorms is ever present even in the more peaceful weather months such as August. Do not attempt this hike on windy days, since the area is famous for high winds. Gusts exceeding 60 miles per hour have been recorded on what otherwise may be a mildly breezy day. Bring along wind gear and raingear, gloves, wool cap, and warm clothing. Carry plenty of water for yourself and your pet.

The great benefit of this hike is that you can test yourself and your pet in difficult, top-of-the-mountain conditions in relative safety. At no time will you be farther than 1.5 miles from your vehicle, so a quick turnaround and return to safety is possible.

Start by hiking up past the Continental Divide sign on the lower trail to reach the gravelly, wide, and well-trodden path that gains the ridge. The trail follows the ridge but there are no sharp drop-offs. You gain almost 1000 feet in the first mile, then the trail levels off. Pass over four rocky knobs that are well cairned. The fifth-highest knob is the summit.

Look for a sign-in register in the wind shelter on the summit. Then, if the weather is good, savor the views. The vistas of ridges upon ridges and peaks upon peaks in every direction are incredible. Interstate 70 is a flimsy thread thousands of feet below you to the north. Beyond it is Woods Mountain (12,940) and just east of it are Mount Parnassus (13,524 feet) and Bard Peak (13,641). Grizzly Peak (13,427 feet) is to the south. Its ridge stretches southeast to the famous Fourteeners, Torreys Peak (14,267 feet) and beyond it Grays Peak (14,270 feet).

Return the way you came.

Loveland Pass summit (Photo by Stefan Krusze)

U.S. HIGHWAY 40 CORRIDOR

43. Mount Flora

Round trip: 5 miles
Hiking time: 6 hours
High point: 13,132 feet
Elevation gain: 1832 feet
Best hiking time: May–September
Maps: USGS Berthoud Pass; Trails Illustrate Winter Park, Central City, Rollins Pass (no. 103)
For more information: Arapaho National Forest, Clear Creek Ranger District, (303) 567-3000

Getting there: Take Interstate 70 from Denver west and exit onto U.S. Highway 40 heading toward Empire. Drive through Empire and observe the speed limit (there is a notorious speed trap in the middle of the town). Continue up the winding road to the summit of Berthoud Pass. Park in the large parking lot on the right. Adjacent to the parking lot is a ski lodge that has a snack bar, souvenir shop, and restrooms. Over the years, endeavors to operate a ski resort on top of the pass have blossomed and faltered.

The Continental Divide Trail (CDT) bisects Berthoud Pass, elevation 11,300 feet, and the entire hike is along the CDT. The Front Range segment of the CDT has been called its crown jewel. Here the trail is at its

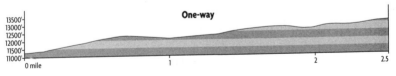

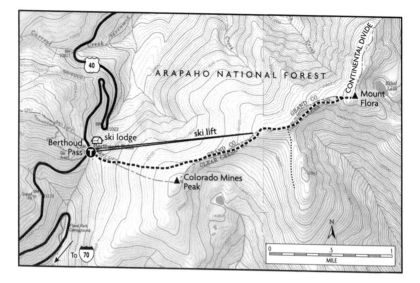

highest elevation along its entire 3000-mile length and skyline hiking offers exceptional panoramas of the spine that divides the flow of water on the North American continent. Because of its location on the CDT, this hike can be extended into a backpack, particularly toward the north, where the trail's alignment is complete.

At 13,132 feet, the summit of Mount Flora is not the highest point of the CDT, but it is one of the highest. The joy is that accessing this hike is easy and the climb itself is mostly over grassy slopes and across tundra abloom with flowers during spring and summer. Mount Flora certainly deserves its name. The tundra is carpeted with clover and wildflowers that include alpine avens, alpine spring beauty, alpine sandwort, and moss campion. The showiest is old-man-of-the-mountain, whose large yellow disk follows the sun. Other flowers you may encounter are saxifrage, alpine wallflower, sky pilot, and the sky-blue columbine, growing in clumps among the boulders near the summit.

Since the trail is above timberline, drawbacks include exposure to Colorado's ever-changing weather. There is also no gurgling stream or alpine lake, so bring along plenty of water for yourself and for your pet (there is one possibility of water in a rather wet section on the west ridge of Mount Flora, where there are several springs seeping to the surface). Your pet can be off-leash, but be certain to keep your dog from chasing ptarmigans or picas that you will meet along the way.

Start hiking up the slope behind the ski lodge and head in a northeasterly, angled direction to the Continental Divide ridge. There is no one trail here, but many indistinct paths. This section is rather steep, and there is scrub vegetation. The terrain levels off once you reach the grassy ridge, and the vistas open in all directions. To your right you will see Colorado Mines Peak (Hike 44) bristling with antennas and buildings. To the left, cairns mark the ridge trail here and it is rather easy to spot as it follows the Continental Divide ridge in a northeasterly direction for 1.2 miles.

As you ascend Mount Flora's west face, you will climb over some minor bumps and the trail will snake among boulders. You may encounter several seeping springs and wet spots on this slope, which your dog will enjoy. Look for cairns and ignore the spur ridge that goes off to your right at 1.3 miles.

Climb up the western face of Mount Flora another 0.5 mile to a false summit. Mount Flora has two summits, so don't be fooled by what looks like the peak. Once on top you will see the true summit 0.3 mile ahead of you. Dip into the saddle and lose a couple hundred feet of elevation, then climb steeply over rather gravelly and rocky terrain to the true summit. Look for the canister that contains the sign-in register among the boulders. If the weather holds and it is still early in the day, luxuriate in the sun and the panoramic vistas.

Return the way you came.

Saxifrage blooms profusely on Mount Flora.

44. Colorado Mines Peak and Blue Lake

Round trip: 3 miles
Hiking time: 2–3 hours
High point: 12,300 feet
Elevation gain: 1600 feet
Best hiking time: June–August
Maps: USGS Berthoud Pass; Trails Illustrate Winter Park, Central City, Rollins Pass (no. 103)
For more information: Arapaho National Forest, Clear Creek Ranger District, (303) 567-3000

Getting there: Take Interstate 70 from Denver west and exit onto U.S. Highway 40 heading toward Empire. Drive through Empire and observe the speed limit (there is a notorious speed trap in the middle of the town). Continue up the winding road to the summit of Berthoud Pass. Park in the large parking lot on the right. Adjacent to the parking lot is a ski lodge that has a snack bar, souvenir shop, and restrooms. Over the years, endeavors to operate a ski resort on top of the pass have blossomed and faltered. The ski lift poles and service road are still in evidence.

Berthoud Pass, elevation 11,300 feet, was discovered in 1861, relatively late in the mapping and exploration of these mountains. The man who discovered this deep notch in the sky-high ridge was Swiss-born engineer Edward Louis Berthoud. His plan was to build a road across the ridge, but he was unable to raise sufficient money. Thus, his idea languished until the road to the north across Rollins Pass was completed in 1873. The Berthoud Pass road was built and paid for by the bustling and silver-rich town of Georgetown that lies to the south.

Colorado Mines Peak (named for the Colorado School of Mines in Golden) lies on the Continental Divide. It is not an impressive mountain

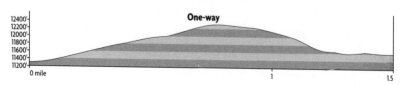

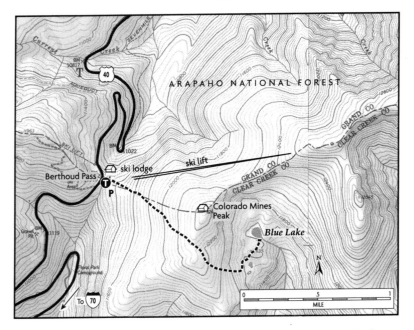

and is topped by several buildings and microwave antennas for telephone transmission. A road winds its way to the summit.

The reason why this is an interesting hike and one suitable for your dog is because the road offers easy access to a delightful, little-known lake that nestles at the foot of the peak's southern slope. The south slope loses snow early and is abloom with wildflowers early in the season. It is also grassy tundra and a joy to walk on.

Start at the south end of the parking lot to pick up the road to the peak and hike east on the road. When you reach timberline, leave the road and contour south across the grassy shoulder of the mountain. There is no trail, so you are going cross-country. When you come to the edge you will look down and see Blue Lake, less than 0.5 mile away but about 800 feet below.

Yes, I think it is worth descending to the lake. Pick the least steep route—there is no marked trail. If you hike this area in early spring, you may find a snowfield and you can glissade down to the lake. The slope, although steep, is free of rocks all the way down to the lake, where there are some boulders.

The lake is surrounded by cinquefoil and willows and patches of soft tundra. The wildflowers on the slope are magnificent in July, especially old-man-of-the-mountain, the stubby sunflower-like plant that turns its face to the sun.

Bistort carpet on a tundra slope of Colorado Mines Peak

Blue Lake is a great place for dogs and children. Your dog will have no problem scrambling back up the slope on the way back, but children might need to be carried.

45. Stanley Mountain

Round trip: 6.5 miles
Hiking time: 6 hours
High point: 12,521 feet
Elevation gain: 1200 feet
Best hiking time: June–August
Maps: USGS Berthoud Pass; Trails Illustrated Winter Park, Central City, Rollins Pass (no. 103)
For more information: Arapaho National Forest, Clear Creek Ranger District, (303) 567-3000

Getting there: Take Interstate 70 from Denver west and exit onto U.S. Highway 40 heading toward Empire. Drive through Empire and observe the speed limit (there is a notorious speed trap in the middle of

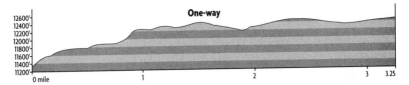

the town). Continue up the winding road to the summit of Berthoud Pass. Park in the large parking lot on the right. Adjacent to the parking lot is a ski lodge that has a snack bar, souvenir shop, and restrooms. Over the years, endeavors to operate a ski resort on top of the pass have blossomed and faltered, but there is a ski lift that usually runs on winter weekends.

This hike follows the Continental Divide Trail (CDT) as it crosses Berthoud Pass and heads west. Stanley Mountain is the first peak to the west of the pass and the entire hike is above timberline. Since weather is always a concern in Colorado, it is best to start the hike early and be off the peak before noon. I was caught on this stretch of the CDT in a nasty thunderstorm that I still remember for the bolts of lightning around me.

A hike on the CDT also lends itself to a backpack, although a longer excursion along a ridgeline requires meticulous preplanning and favorable weather. In addition to packing proper gear, you will need to consult one of the books on the CDT to plan your overnight stops and access to water, in particular if you are hiking with a dog.

Why hike Stanley Mountain with your pet? The going is easy. The trail is well marked. There is minimal scree and the vistas are spectacular.

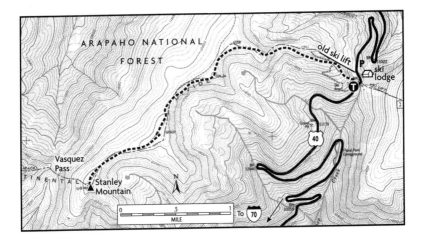

Stanley Mountain in early spring

Cross US 40 and begin hiking on the service road to the left of the defunct ski lift. The going is steep here as you gain the Continental Divide ridge. At 1.5 miles, pass a knoll that may have seeping spring puddles on the west side. Stop here for a rest and let your dog explore the soft tundra terrain.

Continue on the well-defined and cairned trail to the north slope of Stanley Mountain. The top is an easy scramble. The big mountain to the west and separated from you by a deep notch is Vasquez Peak (12,947 feet). The deep notch is Vasquez Pass. If you catch snatches of a distant hum, that is the Henderson Mine, which extracts molybdenum, at the foot of Jones Pass.

Return the way you came.

46. West Fork of Clear Creek

Round trip: 3.5-mile loop
Hiking time: 4–5 hours
High point: 12,400 feet
Elevation gain: 1400 feet
Best hiking time: June–September
Maps: USGS Berthoud Pass; Trails Illustrated Winter Park, Central City, Rollins Pass (no. 103)
For more information: Arapaho National Forest, Clear Creek Ranger District (303) 567-3000

Getting there: Take Interstate 70 from Denver and then take U.S. Highway 40 toward Empire and Winter Park. At 7 miles past Empire (there is an infamous speed trap in this small town), look to the left for a sign that says Jones Pass/Henderson Mine. This sign comes at a hairpin turn that signals the start of the highway's climb up to Berthoud Pass, so keep

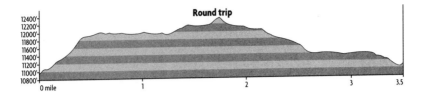

Round trip

an eye out for the turnoff. Cross the highway onto this side road. Continue 2.6 miles until you reach the Henderson Mine turnoff. Bear right and continue up the dirt road for 1.3 miles, following signs for Jones Pass. When you see the sign to the left for Jones Pass ignore it. Continue straight ahead, and enter a broad meadow. The Jones Pass Road veers sharply to your left. Go past the turnoff another few hundred feet

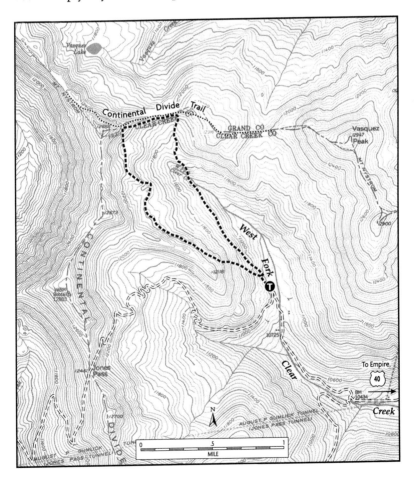

Hiking along Clear Creek

until the road peters out. Park on the gravel shoulder of the road near West Fork Clear Creek on your right.

This hike is a loop of the West Fork Clear Creek drainage. You cannot get lost here since the gully that forms this drainage is narrow and compact. There is no real trailhead and the trail is faint at times. This is National Forest land where your dog can be off-leash while exploring the scents and diversions created by the many rivulets that join at the bottom of the gulch to form the creek. More likely than not you and your dog will be alone for the duration of the hike since this hike is very much off the beaten track.

Cross the road from your car and look for a stand of tall conifers to locate a narrow trail. Follow the trail as it parallels the creek. As you climb out of the gully, the ridge of the Continental Divide will unfold before you. Several cairns mark the trail's progress and the ridge is your destination. It is narrow, but not overly so and following the ridge trail is easy. It is marked well with Continental Divide Trail (CDT) signs. Your dog, even if not used to high places, should not encounter any difficulties, and you only stay on the ridge for a short distance.

Stop on the ridge for a moment and look around. From this vantage point you experience the vastness of the two watersheds of the North American continent. The creek that you have followed up to the ridge flows into Clear Creek, which then flows into the South Platte River, whose waters eventually reach the Missouri River and then flow on to the Mississippi. To the west, the mountain ranges stretch to the horizon and the water that flows off their slopes eventually reaches the Colorado River and the Pacific Ocean.

Since you are above timberline and there is no shelter, watch the weather. After a rest or a snack, follow the clearly defined ridge to the north-northwest, but keep an eye on the bowl you hiked up. The ridge slopes slightly into a saddle as you reach the north side of the bowl. There are several faint trails going down. Select one of them and scramble down the gully, which is covered with scrub vegetation. This side of the gully is less steep than the side you hiked up.

As you reach the bottom of the bowl, traverse to your right (south-southeast) and to the stand of conifers that mark the trail that you used to climb out of the bowl. Pick up the trail and stop at the creek where the banks are shallow, allowing your dog a well-deserved wallow.

Follow the creek back to the road. You will exit the gully about a few hundred feet above your parked vehicle.

47. Butler Gulch

Round trip: 4.5 miles
Hiking time: 3–4 hours
High point: 11,900 feet
Elevation gain: 1500 feet
Best hiking time: May–September, popular snowshoe in winter months
Maps: USGS Berthoud Pass; Trails Illustrate Winter Park, Central City, Rollins Pass (no. 103)
For more information: Arapaho National Forest, Clear Creek Ranger District, (303) 567-3000

Getting there: Take Interstate 70 from Denver and then take U.S. Highway 40 toward Empire and Winter Park. At 7 miles past Empire (there is an infamous speed trap in this small town), look to the left for a sign that says Jones Pass/Henderson Mine. This sign comes at a hairpin turn

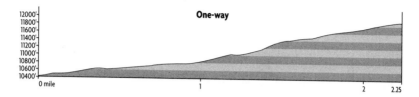

that signals the start of the highway's climb up to Berthoud Pass, so keep
an eye out for the turnoff. Cross the highway onto this side road. Continue 2.6 miles until you reach the Henderson Mine turnoff. Bear right
and drive 0.5 mile and park in the designated area above the mine.

Butler Gulch offers a delightful hike, although starting out you may have
your doubts because of the molybdenum mine. The hike's positive at-
tributes include easy access to water, a long stretch of soft spongy trail,
shade, and an interesting glimpse of Colorado's mining history.

   This hike can easily be extended into an overnight camping adventure. Camp near timberline in the meadow at the head of the gulch. Butler
Creek is a reliable source of water, although you need to purify it if you

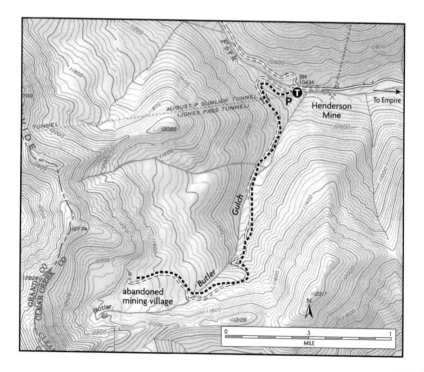

Remains of mining activity in Butler Gulch

do not bring along drinking water. Mountains of the Continental Divide rim the gulch and offer a variety of day trips from a camp base.

From the parking area, head west up the road. Go around a gate and across a high bridge over Clear Creek. Almost at once you will find yourself in a shaded dell and the hum of the mine will quickly die away. The hike follows an old mining road that over the years has been covered with decaying pine needles from the tall ponderosas lining the road. The ground rises slowly and there are plenty of shade-loving flowers and ferns along the way. The trail is wide and has several rivulet crossings your pet will enjoy wallowing in. There is a rock-hop crossing at Butler Creek. There also may be some fallen large logs that you can cross on. Toward the end of the summer, the stream is rather shallow, so if you are not surefooted on wet rocks or logs, you may want to wait until late August to do this hike.

After crossing Butler Creek, the landscape opens up and wildflowers are plentiful as you approach timberline. Here the trail becomes steep as it rises in switchbacks. To the north you can catch a glimpse of Vasquez Peak (12,947 feet), which missed becoming a Thirteener by a mere 53 feet.

The trail enters a wide bowl rimmed by the ridges of the Continental Divide. Pass through meadows filled with Indian paintbrush, chiming bells, arnica, and Parry's primrose as you approach another crossing of Butler Creek, which bisects the bowl. The trail, which has become indistinct now, ends in an abandoned mining village. In bygone days, there were mines in this area as well as several cabins. The ruins of both, including an ancient automobile chassis, offer an interesting diversion.

Return the way you came.

U.S. HIGHWAY 285 CORRIDOR

48. Goose Creek

Round trip: 10 miles
Hiking time: 8 hours
High point: 9200 feet
Elevation gain: 2000 feet
Best hiking time: May–September
Maps: USGS McCurdy Mountain; Trails Illustrated Tarryall Mountains, Kenosha Pass (no. 105)
For more information: Pike National Forest, South Platte Ranger District, (303) 275-5610

Getting there: This is a long drive, but it is worth it. From Denver, drive west on U.S. Highway 285 for 36 miles to Pine Junction. Turn left (south) onto County Road 126 and continue for 21.8 miles. Turn right (south) onto Forest Road 211, which leads to Cheesman Lake. After 2 miles, turn right again (west) at the sign pointing to Goose Creek. Drive 1.1 miles west to a fork in the road. Bear left onto FR 211. Continue 5.2 miles to a road intersection just south of Molly Gulch Campground. Turn right and drive 4.7 miles to the Goose Creek Trail trailhead access road. About half way along this segment, pass Goose Creek Campground. At the trailhead access sign turn right (north) and drive 1.3 miles to the trailhead parking area. There is a large Lost Creek Wilderness sign at

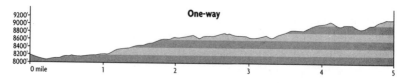

the trailhead. The trailhead area of Goose Creek was affected by the 2002 wildfires in Colorado but not the trail itself.

The Goose Creek Trail provides access into the southeast portion of the Lost Creek Wilderness. Because the trail passes into the wilderness, your dog must be leashed. Although the trail continues for 9.6 miles to the Wigwam Trail, this hikes ends at about 5 miles at the abandoned buildings and the remains of a shaft house. These buildings date to the early 1900s when an attempt was made to build a water reservoir by creating an underground dam on Lost Creek.

Start at a meadow but quickly descend into a lush forest that will stay with you for the rest of the hike. At 0.2 mile, cross the first of several footbridges and boardwalks. Because the peaty soft ground is so

Remains of old buildings at the end of Goose Creek Trail hike

boggy in sections, boardwalks and long footbridges were built to cross the wetter portions. Your dog will have access to water all along the trail. The trail is easy to follow and heads in a general northerly direction.

Just across the first footbridge, Hankins Pass Trail bears left (west) and Goose Creek Trail continues straight ahead (north). At 0.6 mile, you will reach a long metal footbridge that crosses Goose Creek. In another 0.2 mile, the trail crosses a meadow. In another 0.3 mile bear uphill to the right at an unmarked fork. Here comes the elevation gain.

Continue hiking while keeping an eye out for some of the interesting cliff formations in this area. They are to the northwest. One of the better-known landmarks is a thumblike spire. To the right of the thumb you can make out a natural arch in the rocks.

At about 5 miles a sign marks the turnoff to the historic buildings and shaft house remains. This is a good place to stop and rest. A little to the

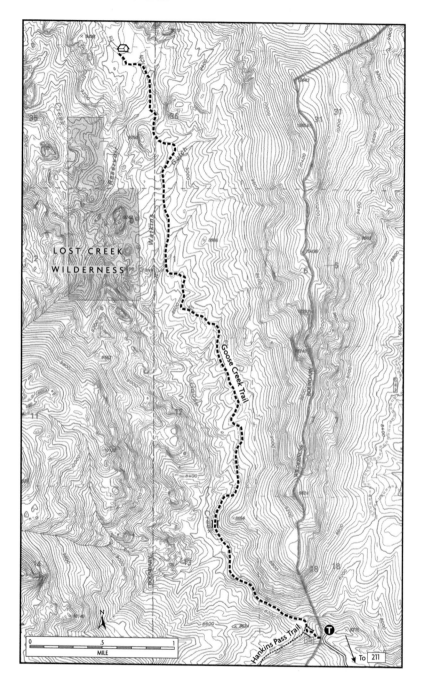

left of the ruins is the creek and some shallow places where your dog can enjoy a good wallow. Return the way you came.

Backpacking: Several camping sites are near the long metal footbridge and hikers also continue past the historic buildings to make a popular backpacking loop. Goose Creek Trail intersects with McCurdy Park Trail at mile 6.5. Turn left and follow it to its intersection with the Brookside Trail. Next, you can head south about 1 mile to the Lake Park Trail and follow it to the Hankins Pass Trail. Hike this trail east back to Goose Creek Trail and trailhead. The total distance of this loop is about 24 miles.

49. Brookside-McCurdy Trail

Round trip: 7 miles
Hiking time: 6 hours
High point: 10,200 feet
Elevation gain: 2200 feet
Best hiking time: May–October
Maps: USGS Shawnee; Trails Illustrated Tarryall Mountains, Kenosha Pass (no. 105)
For more information: Pike National Forest, South Park Ranger District, (719) 836-2031

Getting there: Drive west from Denver on U.S. Highway 285 for 37 miles to the town of Bailey. In the center of Bailey and just past the Conoco gas station, turn left onto County Road 64. There is a blue sign for the County Road 64 intersection just before the Conoco station. Cross the North Fork South Platte River. Pass a lumberyard and houses. Continue past a stop sign to a fork in the road. Bear left on the gravel road and drive 1.5 miles to Payne Gulch, clearly marked on the right. Turn right and continue a few hundred feet to a small parking lot on the left. The trailhead for the Brookside-McCurdy Trail is on the left (also the trailhead for the Payne Creek Trail). Your dog needs to be leashed when you enter the wilderness area.

One-way

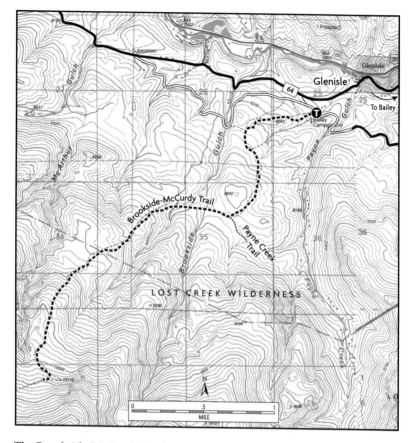

The Brookside-McCurdy Trail is the major north-south trail into the center of the Lost Creek Wilderness in Pike National Forest. The trail extends for nearly 36 miles and reaches an elevation of 11,880 feet. The hike described here starts in Pike National Forest and enters the Lost Creek Wilderness. The trail follows the creek into a deciduous and conifer forest and rises moderately as it heads south into the wilderness area. At higher elevations, vistas open up to the west and small meadows offer pleasant rest and lunch opportunities. Wilderness regulations apply once you cross the boundary, so leash your pet.

From the trailhead, follow the well-marked trail as it rises gently to the first creek crossing at about 1 mile. A second log crossing is a short distance ahead. At about 1.3 miles the Payne Creek Trail veers off to the left. Stay on the Brookside-McCurdy Trail as it continues straight ahead (south).

There are two more stream crossings, one on a plank footbridge and the other over rocks, as the trail climbs out of the Platte River Range. Reach the Lost Creek Wilderness boundary after an elevation gain of 1000 feet. A trapezoidal wooden sign marks the boundary and a wilderness regulations poster is a few feet past it. Once you enter the wilderness, your pet, who may have been walking beside you or sampling the many opportunities for a quick dip and drink, must be leashed.

Once past the wilderness boundary, the trail narrows to follow long,

On the trail into the Lost Creek Wilderness

upward switchbacks. These are occasionally barred by fallen timber, but the trail picks up on the other side of such obstacles and is clearly visible.

Go as far as you wish, gaining another 1200 feet over the next 1.5 miles of steep climbing, to a small meadow with a pleasant view. Make certain your pet has the stamina to handle both the climb and the rock-strewn trail. Lunch at the vista spot, then return the way you came.

Backpacking: This hike can also be done as a long backpack, with camping in the Lost Creek Wilderness. The Brookside-McCurdy Trail continues to climb up and over into Craig Park, where it intersects with the Craig Park Trail. The next segment rises south out of Craig Park over a saddle and then descends into North Lost Park, where it leaves the wilderness area and joins the Colorado Trail. After running together for two miles, the Colorado Trail turns east and north while the Brookside-McCurdy Trail veers south following North Lost Creek to the Lost Park Trailhead.

50. Ben Tyler Trail

Round trip: 10 miles
Hiking time: 9–10 hours or backpack
High point: 11,600 feet
Elevation gain: 3200 feet
Best hiking time: May–July; September–early October
Maps: USGS Shawnee; Trails Illustrated Tarryall Mountains,
   Kenosha Pass (no. 105)
For more information: Pike National Forest, South Park Ranger
   District, (719) 836-2031

Getting there: Take U.S. Highway 285 from Denver west for 38 miles to the hamlet of Shawnee. Go past Shawnee for 2.3 miles. The southbound highway has a passing lane. Just as the passing lane ends, look to your left for a small parking lot and a Forest Service sign. This is the parking lot for the Ben Tyler Trail.

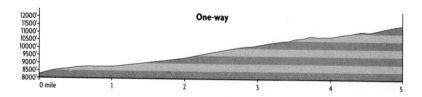

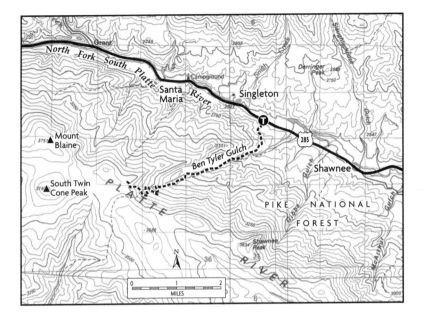

The Ben Tyler Trail is famous for its tight, steep switchbacks, wildflowers in spring and early summer, and a fabulous show of golden aspen in early fall. The trail is strenuous whether as a day hike or a backpack, so you and your pet should be in good shape to hike it.

This is one of the oldest trails in Colorado. It is named after lumberman Ben Tyler who lived with his family in the gulch along a creek that now also bears his name. Tyler made his money by hauling lumber to South Park for the booming town of Fairplay during the gold rush.

Beginning almost at the trailhead itself, the trail climbs steeply in a dozen or so switchbacks. The trail then flattens out and the creek that has been down in the gulch now flows on the left and provides easy access for a wallow or swim for your dog.

When you reach the log bridge on your left over the creek, do not take it. The Ben Tyler Trail continues straight ahead to another stream crossing. The stream now flows on your right. The trail levels off after the crossing and the forest changes to spruce and pine. Occasional meadows provide views to the west of the Kenosha Mountains. The two most prominent peaks are Mount Blaine to the west and South Twin Cone Peak to the southwest.

Snow tends to linger in drifts high up on this trail as late as June. Find a pleasant meadow for lunch before returning the way you came.

Ben Tyler Trail is long and challenging.

Backpacking: The Ben Tyler Trail is suitable for backpacking. It offers excellent camping sites at the top of the valley, beyond the meadows where the day hike ends. The final section of steep switchbacks up the narrowing valley leads to the Craig Park Trail junction that is marked with a Forest Service sign. The Ben Tyler Trail continues to climb, crossing Ben Tyler Creek again, to a high saddle above timberline. If you continue west, you will eventually intersect with the Colorado Trail as it turns northwest to cross Kenosha Pass.

51. Scott Gomer Trail and Abyss Lake Trail

Round trip: 14.6 miles
Hiking time: 12 hours or backpack
High point: 12,650 feet
Elevation gain: 3000 feet
Best hiking time: July–August
Maps: USGS Mount Evans; Trails Illustrated Idaho Springs, Georgetown, Loveland Pass (no. 104)
For more information: Arapaho National Forest, Clear Creek Ranger District, (303) 567-3000; Pike National Forest, South Platte Ranger District, (303) 275-5610

Getting there: From Denver, drive southwest on U.S. Highway 285 approximately 40 miles to Grant. Turn right (north) onto the well-marked Guanella Scenic and Historic Byway. Drive 5 miles to the Scott Gomer

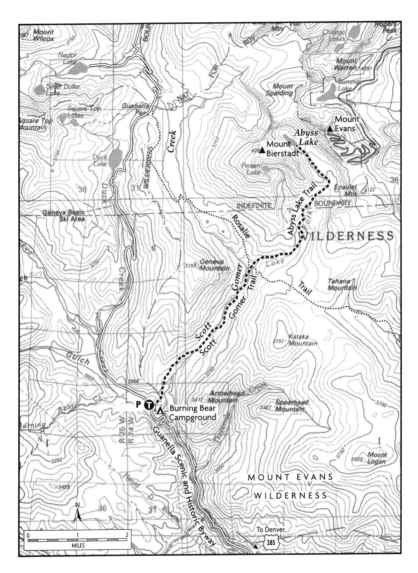

Trail trailhead, on the east (right) side of the road and near the Burning Bear Campground. There is a large parking lot at the trailhead.

This is a difficult, long hike, both because of the distance and the elevation gain. What is great about it is that you can go as far as you want and turn back after having lunch at one of the meadows or several smaller lakes below Abyss Lake. Another plus is that there are many access points

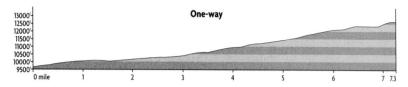

to water for your dog. And because of the distance and difficulty you will likely be alone as you hike deep into the Mount Evans Wilderness, enjoying incredible views as you gain altitude. Scott Gomer Trail intersects with the Rosalie Trail, the major north-south trail through the Mount Evans Wilderness with many opportunities for backpacking.

This hike goes to Abyss Lake, a tarn tucked away in a high glacial cirque between Mount Bierstadt, the sawtooth ridge, and Mount Evans. On the way you may encounter bighorn sheep and mountain goats so keep your dog on a leash, required by wilderness regulations.

From the trailhead, begin hiking northeast on the Scott Gomer Trail that follows Scott Gomer Creek and has several stream crossings, mostly over rocks and logs.

Shortly after the first creek crossing, Mount Bierstadt rises into the sky on your left. After crossing the creek twice more, the trail joins the Rosalie Trail (Hike 34) 3.5 miles from the trailhead. The Rosalie Trail comes in

Hiking in the Mount Evans Wilderness along the Scott Gomer Trail (Photo by Stefan Krusze)

from your left. Follow both trails for a scant 0.04 mile. At this point, the Rosalie Trail veers right (south) while the main trail, now the Abyss Lake Trail, bears slightly to the left.

In less than 0.5 mile pass a small lake on your right. The Abyss Lake Trail ascends to a second larger lake on your left at 6.6 miles. The trail rises now in steep switchbacks.

This is where the willows begin and the trail turns northwest as it skirts the lake. A creek that drains from Abyss Lake will be on your left. Abyss Lake is 0.7 mile ahead of you. Don't be fooled by a smaller lake just below Abyss Lake and on your left. The trail ends at Abyss Lake and the sheer cliffs behind it.

Return the way you came.

52. Three Mile Creek Trail

Round trip: 12 miles
Hiking time: 7 hours
High point: 12,000 feet
Elevation gain: 2900 feet
Best hiking time: June–October
Maps: USGS Mount Logan; USGS Mount Evans; Trails Illustrated
   Idaho Springs, Georgetown, Loveland Pass (no. 104)
For more information: Pike National Forest, South Platte Ranger
   District, (303) 275-5610

Getting there: From Denver, drive southwest on U.S. Highway 285 approximately 40 miles to Grant. Turn right (north) onto the well-marked Guanella Scenic and Historic Byway. Drive 2.5 miles to the trailhead on the right (east) side of the road.

This hike along Three Mile Creek is through a dense deciduous and conifer forest and has multiple stream crossings. These crossings are shallow and often no more than a large step across to the other bank. Dogs love this hike.

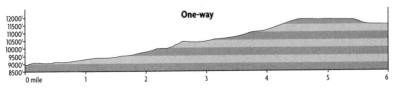

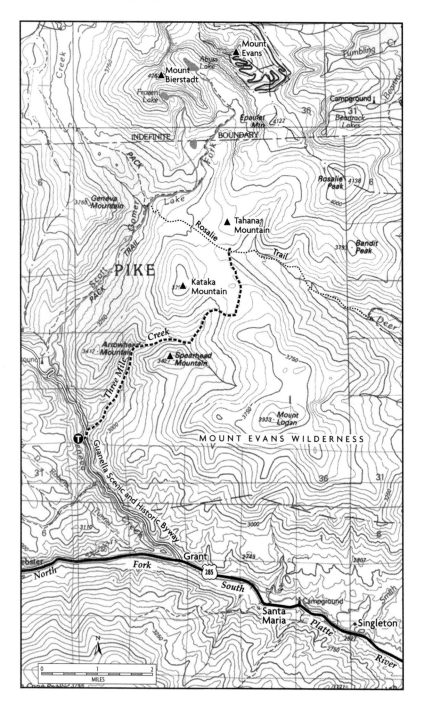

Three Mile Creek offers a shaded trail through an aspen forest. (Photo by Stefan Krusze)

It's a favorite Colorado Mountain Club doggie hike. The hike also offers spectacular autumn foliage and high mountain scenery at timberline.

Since the Three Mile Creek drainage begins in the southern half of the Mount Evans Wilderness, wilderness rules apply and your dog must be leashed. Because the Three Mile Creek Trail penetrates deep into the Mount Evans Wilderness and intersects with the Rosalie Trail, this day hike can easily become a one- or two-night backpack with camping in one of the many meadows inside the wilderness area.

From the trailhead, the first 3 miles of the trail follow Three Mile Creek in a northeasterly direction up a narrow drainage canyon. When the trail swings east as it approaches timberline, the forest thins and meadows offer glimpses of the surrounding mountains.

At a point east of Spearhead Mountain, the trail leaves the creek and ascends steeply in a sequence of switchbacks. At the top of the ridge, the trail turns north again, the forest thins, and you emerge into a series of timberline meadows.

Kataka Mountain is to the left (west) and Mount Evans and Mount Bierstadt rise majestically ahead and slightly to the left (northwest). Continue north to the intersection with the Rosalie Trail (Hike 34). There is a nice meadow in this area for a rest or lunch.

Return the way you came.

53. Kenosha Pass East

Round trip: 14 miles
Hiking time: 8–9 hours
High point: 10,500 feet
Elevation gain: 1300 feet
Best hiking time: May–June; September–October
Maps: USGS Jefferson; Trails Illustrated Tarryall Mountains, Kenosha Pass (no. 105)
For more information: Pike National Forest, South Park Ranger District, (719) 836-2031

Getting there: Take U.S. Highway 285 from Denver west for 68 miles to Kenosha Pass. Pull off on your left onto a dirt road just as a rail fence ends on your left. Continue to a parking area near toilets and picnic tables.

This trail is a wonderful aspen-season hike when the leaves turn a glowing yellow. But be warned, it is a well-known destination and you and your pet may encounter many other hikers, especially on weekends. The

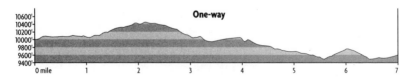

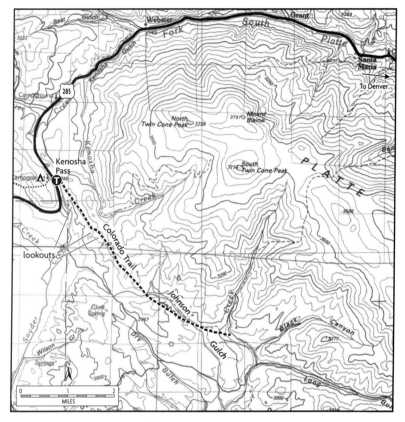

good news is that in less than 2 miles, the crowds thin out considerably. The hike is along a segment of the Colorado Trail (CT), which starts in Waterton Canyon in Jefferson County and continues across the state to Durango. Thus, you can easily make this hike into a backpack, exploring the CT in either direction.

Walk to the south edge of the parking lot to the Colorado Trail trailhead. You will immediately enter an aspen forest of mature trees with thick white trunks. Hike in a southeasterly direction on an old jeep road that rises gently. The jeep road continues along the broad unnamed ridge with recurring meadows that offer panoramic views of the South Park basin. There are also large display boards describing the vegetation and history of the area.

After 1 mile, angle right onto another jeep road and enter stands of aspen and bristlecone pine. At 2 miles descend to another jeep road. The way is well marked by posts with the Colorado Trail logo. At about 3 miles,

An old road forms part of the trail through aspen forest on Kenosha Pass.

look for a seasonal stream in Johnson Gulch. A wide grassy meadow is next and this may be a good place to lunch or turn around.

The trail drops slowly as it approaches Rock Creek in 1 mile, and you pass a red cattle gate. Continue a short distance until you reach Rock Creek and the junction with the Rock Creek Trail. Let your pet have a well-deserved wallow before returning the way you came.

You may encounter cattle grazing in this area since the Rock Creek Cow Camp is nearby and cattle are driven into this area for summer grazing from ranches in South Park.

54. Kenosha Pass West

Round trip: 10 miles
Hiking time: 6–7 hours
High point: 10,300 feet
Elevation gain: 1600 feet
Best hiking time: May–June; September–October
Maps: USGS Jefferson; Trails Illustrated Tarryall Mountains, Kenosha Pass (no. 105)
For more information: Pike National Forest, South Park Ranger District, (719) 836-2031

Getting there: Take U.S. Highway 285 from Denver west for 68 miles to Kenosha Pass. Pull off on your right (north side of the road) and park

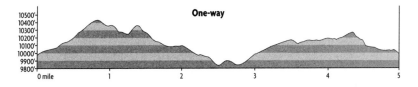

near the Kenosha Pass summit sign. Parking past the fence is restricted for Kenosha Campground users.

This hike can also be done one-way with a car shuttle. To leave a car at the other end of the trail, drive south past Kenosha Pass for about 5 miles to the town of Jefferson and turn right on Jefferson Lake Road, which is clearly marked. Drive 2 miles, turn right, and follow signs for Jefferson Lake. Continue for 3 miles. Look for a wooden sign on the right that shows Colorado Trail mileage to Kenosha Pass to the right and to Georgia Pass to the left. Pull off on the shoulder and leave one car. The Jefferson Creek Recreation Area has campsites as well as picnic areas.

Like the preceding hike (Hike 53), this hike is along the Colorado Trail and along the ridgeline sloping from Kenosha Pass. As the trail passes through a succession of deciduous forest copses and meadows, it makes several stream crossings that offer opportunities for your dog to get wet

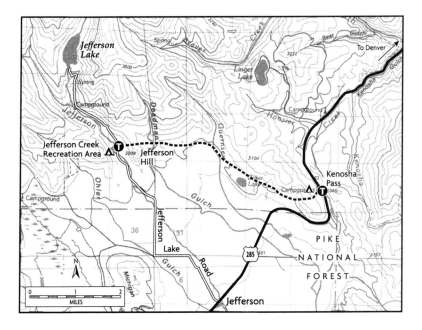

Vista of the Mosquito Range from Kenosha Pass

and to lap water. The trail is not rocky and at times you and your dog can walk side by side.

Starting from Kenosha Pass, locate the Colorado Trail trailhead at the northwest side of the large campground parking area and immediately enter a mature forest of aspen.

In less than a mile the noise of traffic fades as the trail descends the ridge and passes through a series of rolling meadows that open to panoramic vistas of South Park and the Fourteeners of the Mosquito Range. Cross an old logging road and continue on the trail to Guernsey Creek, which you cross on huge logs. Here your pet can enjoy the shallow stream bed.

There is another stream crossing at about 4 miles, over Deadman Creek, again on large logs. To your left you will see Jefferson Hill, but the trail skirts the rounded hump.

Cross a streamlet on rocks at about 4.5 miles and ascend a low ridge before reaching a livestock gate. Be careful of the single barbed wire fence on either side. Pass through the gate and descend 0.5 mile to the Jefferson Lake Road where you can relax at a picnic area nearby.

Pick up your second car or return the way you came on the trail.

55. Georgia Pass

One-way: 5 miles
Hiking time: 4 hours
High point: 11,800 feet
Elevation loss: 1800 feet
Best hiking time: May–October
Maps: USGS Jefferson; Trails Illustrated Tarryall Mountains,
    Kenosha Pass (no. 105)
For more information: Pike National Forest, South Park Ranger
    District, (719) 836-2031

Getting there: Take U.S. Highway 285 from Denver west for 73 miles
to the town of Jefferson and turn right on Jefferson Lake Road, which
is clearly marked. Drive 2 miles and turn right and follow signs for
Jefferson Lake. Continue for 3 miles. Look for a wooden sign on the right
that shows Colorado Trail mileage to Kenosha Pass to the right and to
Georgia Pass to the left. Pull off on the shoulder and leave one vehicle
here, if doing this hike as a shuttle (recommended). You can also continue a few hundred feet and park at the Beaver Ponds Picnic Grounds.
The trail is in the Jefferson Creek Recreation Area.

To reach the Georgia Pass trailhead, return 3 miles to the turnoff from
Jefferson Lake Road. Turn right and drive 2 miles. Bear right on County
Road 54, also called Michigan Creek Road. The road is paved for several
miles, then becomes gravel as it begins to climb to Georgia Pass.
    To reach Georgia Pass directly from U.S. Highway 285, look for Michi-
gan Creek Road and turn right. Continue on this road for 12 miles as it
climbs to Georgia Pass. Just before the pass the road becomes very rough
and is called Glacier Ridge Road. Continue to the sign that indicates the
Colorado Trail (CT) crossing and park nearby. High clearance vehicles are
recommended on the access road.
    Georgia Pass is on the grassy ridge of the Continental Divide and the
imposing sharp cone to the west is Mount Guyot. Pick up the Colorado

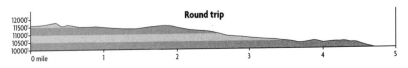

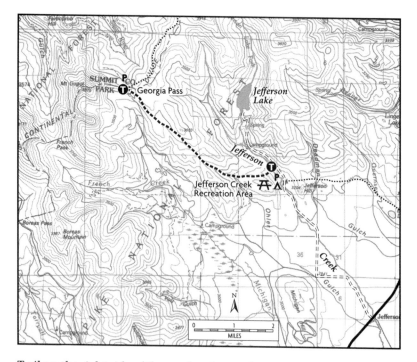

Trail on the right side of the road and ascend on a rocky trail for 0.2 mile to a saddle. From here on the hike is downhill.

Hike in a southeasterly direction across the tundra. At 1 mile, cross the North Jefferson Trail that goes off to the left (northeast). In another 0.5 mile look for stunted trees bent by prevailing winds. Beyond these trees lies timberline and the trail enters a spruce forest. From here on down, the trail is continuously forested and the ground is often spongy, a pleasant relief for your dog.

Since the Colorado Trail is open to bikers in this area, keep a sharp lookout for them and keep your dog at your side to avoid trail mishaps.

Descend on several switchbacks the southeast side of the broad, forested ridge. Pass several small clearings along the way that bloom well into the season with yellow arnica, a star-shaped wildflower with heart-shaped leaves.

At about 4.5 miles, cross an old road and begin a gradual descent on switchbacks into a gully that drops into the Jefferson Creek drainage.

The trail becomes an old jeep road and crosses a seasonal creek. Just before the end of the hike, cross Jefferson Creek on a wooden plank bridge. Your pet can enjoy a well-deserved wallow here.

Pick up your first car at Jefferson Lake Road and return to Georgia Pass for your other vehicle.

Like the two preceding hikes (Hikes 53 and 54), this hike is also along the Colorado Trail, which begins at Waterton Canyon south of Denver and ends in Durango. The CT stretches nearly 500 miles as it crosses eight mountain ranges, seven national forests, and six wilderness areas. Backpacking and extended hiking opportunities are possible in either direction from Georgia Pass.

Georgia Pass summit view

STEAMBOAT SPRINGS

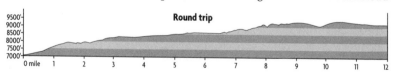

56. Service Creek Trail

One-way: 12 miles
Hiking time: 10 hours or backpack
High point: 9400 feet
Elevation gain: 2400 feet
Best hiking time: July–August
Maps: USGS Blacktail Mountain; Trails Illustrated Steamboat
    Springs, Rabbit Ears Pass (no. 118)
For more information: Routt National Forest, Yampa Ranger District,
    (970) 638-4516

Getting there: From Steamboat Springs, drive 10 miles east on U.S. Highway 40 to County Road 131 and turn right (you can only make a right turn). County Road 131 jogs, then heads south for 9 miles to the intersection with County Road 18. Turn left (east) and drive 12 miles south on County Road 18. When you come to a fork, bear left. The right fork goes to Stagecoach State Park and Reservoir. Continue past the Stagecoach turnoff for approximately 1.7 miles to Service Creek State Wildlife Area and turn right. Follow the main road 0.5 mile to the Service Creek Trail trailhead and parking lot near the Yampa River.

To reach the Buffalo Park trailhead, follow U.S. Highway 40 to Rabbit Ears Pass. About 1 mile before the pass, look to the right for Buffalo Park Road

Round trip

9500'
9000'
8500'
8000'
7500'
7000'

0 mile   1   2   3   4   5   6   7   8   9   10   11   12

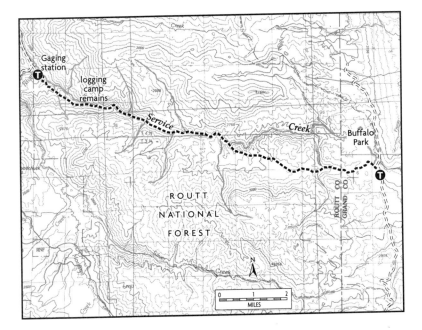

(Forest Road 100). Turn right (south) and continue for about 18 miles to the trailhead on the right at Buffalo Park.

The north end of the Gore Range, also known as the Park Range, does not draw as many hikers as the mountain ranges easily accessible either by Interstate 70 or by U.S. Highway 285, the two corridors into the Rocky Mountains from metropolitan Denver. Thus, this area remains isolated and primitive with old logging flumes and homesteaders' cabins and trails that bear names with historical references. Service Creek, for example, is called Sarvis Creek on old maps. This name derives from the Sarvis Timber Company that logged this area in the years around 1910.

Service Creek Trail follows Service Creek as it rushes past to empty into the Yampa River. The trail, on the other hand, winds leisurely through dense forests and past relics of logging activity. Since the trail never leaves the creek, numerous opportunities exist for your dog to get wet and hydrate during this long hike.

This is big-game country, so keep a close eye on your dog so he does not confront moose, elk, a big cat, or a black bear. This trail enters the Sarvis Creek Wilderness, so leash regulations apply. In this remote area you and your dog need to go prepared for any eventuality, from bad weather to confronting a moose. A compass and a topographic map are musts on this hike, as well as a full complement of gear for backcountry hiking.

From the parking area at Yampa River, the trail rises out of the river valley on a steep incline to reach Service Creek canyon and then swings southeast. After passing through an aspen forest, the trail enters a spruce-fir forest where the air is aromatic and the terrain is soft from deposits of decaying evergreen needles.

Now, 400 feet above the Yampa drainage, the trail flattens for a short distance and continues to a bridge crossing over Service Creek at 2.2 miles from the trailhead. Nearby are remains of the Sarvis Timber logging camp. Flumes would send the logs downstream to Yampa River. You may want to turn around here if you are on a day hike.

At 2.6 miles, you will encounter a rocky area where the creek runs underground for several hundred yards. Continue to an abandoned cabin on the other side of the creek at 3.4 miles.

Beyond the cabin, the trail's direction is more southerly than easterly and the forest yields to a series of meadows at 6 miles. These meadows stretch for about 0.5 mile and offer a great place for a break for you and your dog, who must be as tired as you are by now. If you are not hiking one-way or backpacking, this is the second place where, after a pleasant rest, you can turn around.

A variety of wildflowers bloom in the meadows along Service Creek.

The trail ascends again, passing through a series of small parks along the stream's edge. At 7.5 miles the trail finally leaves the main drainage and crosses lodgepole pine–covered hills and a series of beaver ponds and lodges. The trail ends in a dirt road as you enter Buffalo Park where it connects with Buffalo Park Road (Forest Road 100).

If you decided to do this hike as an overnight backpack, consider camping after you have passed the beaver ponds or in the vicinity of Buffalo Park. The Routt National Forest extends from north central Colorado to Wyoming and offers numerous backpack opportunities.

57. Fishhook Lake, Lost Lake, and Lake Elmo

Round trip: 6 miles
Hiking time: 4 hours
High point: 10,050 feet
Elevation gain: 600 feet
Best hiking time: June–September
Maps: USGS Mount Werner; Trails Illustrated Steamboat Springs
(no. 118)
For more information: Routt National Forest, Hahn's Peak/Bears Ears
Ranger District, (970) 879-1870

Getting there: From Steamboat Springs, drive U.S. Highway 40 toward Rabbit Ears Pass. As you approach the pass, look for the Dumont Lake Campground turnoff. Follow the road past the campground and picnic area. Turn left at the stone Rabbit Ears Pass monument and follow signs to Forest Road 311, a rough road best suited for a four-wheel-drive vehicle. Follow this road for approximately 4.5 miles to the Base Camp trailhead on the right.

On USGS quads, this trail is called by various names: Wyoming Trail, Jeep Trail, Stock Driveway, and Fireline Trail. More recently this trail

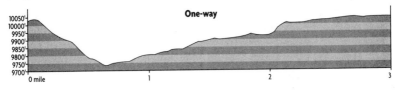

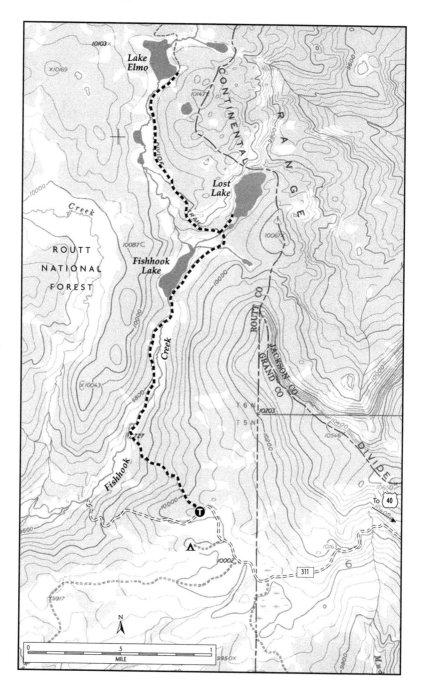

On the trail to three lakes

has become a segment of the Continental Divide Trail that starts in Canada and runs along the backbone of the North American continent to Mexico, a distance of more than 3000 miles.

The trail also extends for 20 miles inside the Mount Zirkel Wilderness where leash laws prevail. This hike follows a little over 3 miles of this very old trail. This section of trail does not run on the ridge of the Continental Divide but rather is on its west side in the valley. It leads to three lakes, with Lake Elmo 3 miles from the trailhead.

The historic antecedents of the Wyoming Trail date to circa 1910, when the trail was used by sheep ranchers in Rawlins, Wyoming, to drive sheep to sales in Steamboat Springs. Later, the trail was used to drive sheep to summer pasture in the Routt National Forest. The grazing allotments have since been cut back or discontinued. Today, the trail is mostly used for hiking.

The hike starts easily enough, a price that will be paid on the climb back up at the end of the day. Shortly after the trailhead, the trail descends 300 feet in 0.5 mile into a meadow that is part of a broad valley. The trail runs next to Fishhook Creek. After crossing the meadow, the trail fords the creek at a point where it is narrow and shallow (good access for your dog).

Next, the trail enters a spruce and fir forest and begins to climb. The Continental Divide is on the right as you hike parallel to it. The trail levels off and dips as it approaches boggy meadows where moose can be seen occasionally. Keep a close eye on your dog here, since the scents he is picking up are tantalizing.

After a 1.4-mile jaunt, the trail reaches Fishhook Lake. This is an oblong-shaped lake nestled amid rolling meadows filled with wildflowers. Continue on the trail along the east side of the lake. Reenter the forest and about 0.3 mile up the trail reach an intersection.

Take the right fork to get to Lost Lake. This is an easy detour since Lost Lake is only a few hundred feet farther on. Before reaching the lake, the trail passes through a spruce and fir forest and past a marshy area overgrown with willows. The lake is rimmed by forests and is a popular camping and fishing spot.

After both you and your dog have taken a break, and played a game of fetch in the lake if there are no nearby anglers, retrace your steps to the intersection of the main trail. Take the left fork and continue to Lake Elmo. The trail to Lake Elmo is well marked and flat.

Return the way you came.

Views of the Continental Divide along the trail

SUMMIT COUNTY

58. Straight Creek

Round trip: 4 miles
Hiking time: 3 hours
High point: 12,900 feet
Elevation gain: 1700 feet
Best hiking time: July–August
Maps: USGS Loveland Pass; Trails Illustrated Idaho Springs, Georgetown, Loveland Pass (no. 104)
For more information: White River National Forest, Dillon Ranger District, (970) 468-5400

Getting there: Take Interstate 70 from Denver west and go through the Eisenhower Tunnel. Once you exit the tunnel, turn right into a small parking area. Look for a paved road that leads north from the parking area. Follow that road and park on the shoulder in sight of a metal ramp across the road. The trailhead is just past the ramp, on the left (north) side of the road.

Why would anyone want to hike amid the traffic noise of the interstate and the loud hum of the ventilators that circulate air in the tunnel? There are two reasons. If you and your pet have been traveling for a while, your pet may have become antsy. Instead of pulling off on the shoulder of the interstate and risking danger, pull off here and go for a short hike.

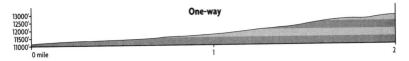

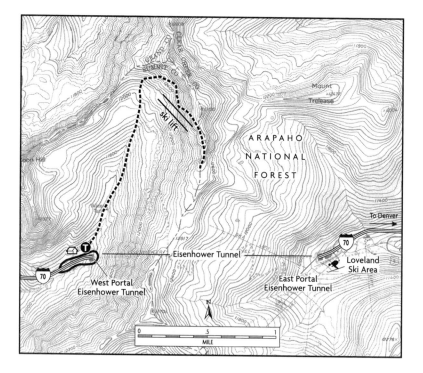

The second reason for hiking Straight Creek is that the creek flows leisurely from the Continental Divide and creates a swampy, peaty gully in which wildflowers thrive. The hike has numerous stream crossings but these are across streamlets and rivulets that can be breached in one long stride. Believe it or not, the roar of the traffic and the hum of the ventilators disappears in about 10 minutes and the enchantment of luxuriant flowers takes over. I have been told that 100 species of wildflowers thrive in this modest gully that faces south and offers the moisture and sunlight flowers need to put on a spectacular show.

Your pet will enjoy the peaty, soft ground and the numerous opportunities to get his paws wet or to wallow in the gently flowing water.

Ignore the giant air intake drums on your right and stay to your left. Hike north along the creek on a mostly discernable wide trail that was once a wagon road. Occasionally, the trail narrows and sections may have been washed out by the previous winter's snow. Some of the wildflowers that grow on this steep hillside are the reddish king's crown, pink elephants, pinkish queen's crown, cowbane, blue columbine, the scarlet paintbrush, and the vivid reddish Parry's primrose.

As you gain altitude, clumps of blue sky pilot grow amid small boulders. The trail becomes a bit vague here, but follow the natural chute upward to the ridge, which is on your right. Veer east to ascend to the Continental Divide. More than 1000 feet below you are the bores that funnel traffic under the monumental ridge of mountains.

Here you will encounter another segment of the old wagon road and the more modern signs of the Loveland Ski Area lifts. Turn right (south) and walk as far as you wish while enjoying the panoramic views. Look west to locate the cross on the Mount of the Holy Cross (14,005 feet). To the south and east are Mount Sniktau (13,234 feet), Grizzly Peak (13,427 feet), Torreys Peak (14,267 feet), and Grays Peak (14,270 feet).

This section above the Eisenhower Tunnel on the Continental Divide is interesting for another reason. This ridge forms Colorado's only land bridge from north to south across I-70.

Return the way you came.

A profusion of water-loving flowers cover Straight Creek's banks.

59. Chihuahua Gulch and Lake

Round trip: 6.1 miles
Hiking time: 6 hours
High point: 12,400 feet
Elevation gain: 1800 feet
Best hiking time: Late July–August
Maps: USGS Montezuma; USGS Grays Peak; Trails Illustrated Idaho
    Springs, Georgetown, Loveland Pass (no. 104)
For more information: White River National Forest, Dillon Ranger
    District, (970) 468-5400

Getting there: Take Interstate 70 west to Loveland Pass/U.S. Highway 6, exit 216, which is the last exit before the Eisenhower Tunnel. Take U.S. 6 over Loveland Pass. Go past the Arapahoe Ski Basin on your left and watch for a turnoff sign on the left for Montezuma. Turn onto Montezuma Road and drive past outlying parking areas for the Keystone Ski Resort. Bear left on Montezuma Road and continue for 4.6 miles to a dirt parking lot and turnoff for Peru Creek Road (Forest Road 260) on the left. If the road is closed to cars because of flooding or a washout, park here. A four-wheel drive does best on Peru Creek Road, which leads to the Chihuahua Gulch Trail trailhead. A passenger car can make the trip with caution. Look for the pullout and the trailhead after passing an old mine on the left, about 2 miles from the bridge over Peru Creek. There is parking for about four vehicles on the right side of the road.

If you were to continue on Montezuma Road, you would shortly reach the old mining town of Montezuma. Founded in the 1860s, Montezuma was one of the silver mining towns and the area is dotted with abandoned mines. Today, Montezuma is inhabited year-round, and it has new vacation homes and a couple bed-and-breakfast inns on the outskirts. It also has a general store on the main street, which remains unpaved, and a fire station. Montezuma lies 5 miles east of Keystone.

The best time to visit this area is definitely after the spring runoff (or

One-way

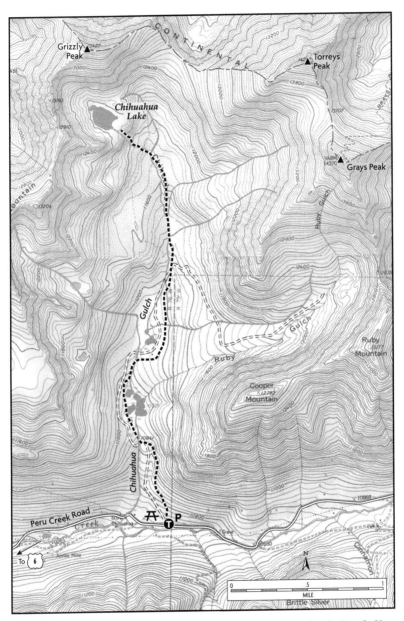

after a dry spell) to avoid possible flooding on Peru Creek Road. You should also bring along an old pair of sneakers and a towel, since the trail has several shallow creek crossings and wading is usually the best way to get across.

But with a name like Chihuahua Gulch, how can a dog lover not hike it or a dog not explore it? Begin hiking on the old mining road that climbs steeply as it passes through groves of aspen. At a fork, bear left, enter a meadow, and make the first creek ford, then follow the road and the creek through a large meadow that has two more stream crossings. Several small ponds are on the right (east). You may want to stop here to rest or for lunch. From here, the old mining road begins to climb in earnest.

The road swings to the right and enters another meadow with more ponds. Cross the creek one more time.

Approximately 2 miles from the trailhead you will come to an old rail fence. Take the trail to the left and leave the road, which peters out farther on. The trail is a steep scramble up a grass and talus slope to Chihuahua Lake, which is left (west) of the trail as you reach the end of the gulch. The lake lies at the base of Grizzly Peak (13,427 feet). Torreys Peak (14,267 feet) and Grays Peak (14,270 feet) are to the right (east).

Return the way you came.

Doggie rest in Chihuahua Gulch

60. McCullough Gulch

Round trip: 2.8 miles
Hiking time: 2 hours
High point: 11,921 feet
Elevation gain: 820 feet
Best hiking time: June–October
Maps: USGS Breckenridge; Trails Illustrated Breckenridge, Tennessee
Pass (no. 109)
For more information: White River National Forest, Dillon Ranger
District, (970) 468-5400

Getting there: From Denver, drive west on Interstate 70 for 70 miles to exit 203, Breckenridge/Frisco. Take Colorado Highway 9 south to Breckenridge. Drive through Breckenridge and zero your odometer at the last traffic light south of town at Boreas Pass Road. Drive for 7.1 miles, passing the small town of Blue River. At 7.1 miles, look for Blue Lakes Road and turn right (west). Drive about 100 yards and turn right (north) on McCullough Gulch Road, a dirt road. Continue for 1.5 miles, bearing left at the fork to the end of the road where there is a gate and a parking area.

If you have ever climbed Quandary Peak (14,265 feet) to bag a Fourteener and have looked to the northeast and down, you probably saw Upper Blue Reservoir as one of the turquoise drops far below. Near the reservoir are picturesque falls that are a popular day excursion. Most hikers (and bikers) end their hike here. However, the trail continues upward for another 1.2 miles, climbing to a tarn at 12,955 feet. Attempt this second leg of the hike when the skies are cloudless, since you will be above timberline all the way up. If you do hike to the tarn, a topographic map is essential (Trails Illustrated recommended). Bring mosquito repellent if hiking in July and August.

In the shadow of the formidable bulk of Quandary Peak to the south and Pacific Peak to the west, this hike in the lowlands starts out simply

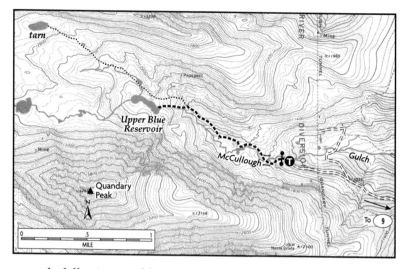

enough, following an old mining road. What is nice about this is that you and your canine companion can walk side by side. This is a pleasure to be savored, since most trails are narrow footpaths. Follow your dog's gaze when his body stiffens suddenly and perhaps you can catch sight of what his keen sight and sensitive nose have already spotted.

The trailhead is at 11,102 feet, next to a gate across the road. Pass the gate on the side and then cross a bridge over roaring McCullough Creek. Continue on the road that is bordered by private property and abandoned mining ventures. It is imperative that your dog stays next to you: use a leash or make sure he is under voice command.

About 0.25 mile into the hike, bear left onto a footpath while the mining road turns right onto private property. The footpath continues for about 1 mile, crossing half a dozen small streams that flow into the gorge created by McCullough Creek.

Soon the roar of falling water draws you to the series of cascades that are tumbling down from the reservoir above. The cascades create an arresting picture of black rock and foaming white water. Near the tumult, scarlet Parry's primrose and other water-loving wildflowers thrive. Early in the season look for marsh marigolds.

Various footpaths lead to the cascades. After exploring several, return to the main trail and hike a little farther to the reservoir itself. It is long and narrow in the middle with a curved shoreline on the far (east) end. The views of the Tenmile Range and the Continental Divide are quite

Sturdy log crossing over McCullough Creek (Photo by Yue Savage)

wonderful here and this is a perfect place for lunch as well as for your dog to take a pleasant dip.

Turn around here and return the way you came, or continue to the tarn on the 12,000-foot shelf if the weather bodes well. Continue on a trail along the north shore of the reservoir and then follow the trail as it runs alongside the north side of the creek, which is on your left. The distance to the tarn is 1.2 miles and the additional elevation gain is 1100 feet. Aside from the spectacular views to the west down the Blue River valley, you and your dog will most likely be alone as you hike up the tundra and rocky terrain.

61. Crystal Lakes

Round trip: 8 miles
Hiking time: 8 hours
High point: 12,971 feet
Elevation gain: 2755 feet
Best hiking time: June–August
Maps: USGS Breckenridge; Trails Illustrated Breckenridge, Tennessee Pass (no. 109)
For more information: White River National Forest, Dillon Ranger District, (970) 468-5400

Getting there: From Denver, drive west on Interstate 70 for 70 miles to exit 203, Breckenridge/Frisco. Drive Colorado Highway 9 south to Breckenridge. Drive through Breckenridge and zero your odometer at

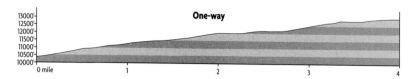

the last traffic light south of town at Boreas Pass Road. Drive 2.5 miles.
A lake called the Goose Pasture Tarn will be on your left. Look on the
right for a sign, "The Crown," which is the name of a subdivision. Turn
right (west) here onto Spruce Creek Road past the houses, bearing left
and heading south. Keep on this road. The trailhead is 1.3 miles from
the point where you turned off Highway 9.

The trail begins at 10,400 feet just below timberline and takes you past
numerous lush alpine meadows abloom with wildflowers from June
through September. Tributaries of nearby Crystal Creek often cross the
trail in streamlets and rivulets that a big step will cross and your dog will
love to sample. The access to flowing water throughout the hike makes
it an ideal hike for a dog, especially if you and your canine companion
are hiking on a hot Colorado summer day.

This is an interesting area historically, since it was the site of frantic placer
gold mining activity in the 1880s. There are several abandoned mines and
cabins along the trail and the trail itself is at times an old mining road. Since
most of this hike is above timberline, start out early to avoid the unpredict-
able Colorado weather and possible thunderstorms early in the afternoon.

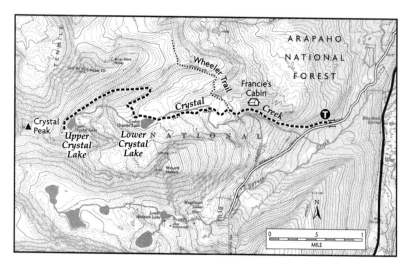

The hike starts on an old mining road that heads due west. Cross Crystal Creek and bear left on the old rough road. Continue along the north side of Crystal Creek on rising terrain through a conifer forest. Pass into a meadow as the trees thin. Climb more steeply past a stand of spruce.

At 1.2 miles, come to the junction with the Wheeler Trail that runs north. Nearby is an old cabin called Francie's Cabin. A Forest Service sign says that dogs are not welcome inside.

Lower Crystal Lake (11,980 feet) is less than 1 mile to the west on a well-defined trail across the tundra. Stop at the lake to enjoy the outstanding views of the Tenmile Range. Crystal Peak (13,858 feet) is due west, rising beyond Upper Crystal Lake, your next destination.

After your dog has enjoyed the water and perhaps a snack, press on, climbing tight switchbacks up to the upper lake at 12,860 feet. It lies on a shelf at the base of Crystal Peak. Check the weather as you hike so that a thunderstorm does not arrive unexpectedly. A cabin at the lake offers some shelter in the event of a storm.

Upper Crystal Lake is surrounded by willows and boulders, with wildflowers blooming where they can. Although many hikers use the trail, few climb the extra 1000 feet to reach the upper lake, so you may enjoy solitude as you admire the fantastic views downvalley.

Return the way you came. Or you can ascend Crystal Peak (the

Crystal Peak dominates the hike to Crystal Lakes.

eighty-second-highest mountain in Colorado) from the lake by scrambling across the talus to the saddle between Crystal Peak and Peak 10.

62. Meadow Creek Trail

Round trip: 9 miles to Eccles Pass; 3 miles to Lily Pad Lakes
Hiking time: 8–9 hours to Eccles Pass; 1.5 hours to Lily Pad Lakes
High point: 11,900 feet at Eccles Pass; 9400 feet at Lily Pad Lakes
Elevation gain: 2700 feet to Eccles Pass; 200 feet to Lily Pad Lakes
Best hiking time: June–October
Maps: USGS Frisco; Trails Illustrated Vail, Frisco, Dillon (no. 108)
For more information: White River National Forest, Dillon Ranger
   District, (970) 468-5400

Getting there: From Denver, drive west on Interstate 70 for 70 miles to exit 203/Breckenridge/Frisco. Take the exit ramp to the traffic circle on the north side of I-70. Continue around on the circle to the gravel road with the Forest Service sign and turn right, taking this gravel frontage road west. Go to the end of the road and park in a lot at the Meadow Creek Trail trailhead.

You have a choice of two hikes at this trailhead: a short, pleasant hike to Lily Pad Lakes or an all-day, strenuous hike into the Eagles Nest Wilderness to Eccles Pass. Both hikes are particularly enjoyable in September when aspen are turning to their spectacular gold color. The Eccles Pass destination is in the Eagles Nest Wilderness, so your dog must be on leash. This also means that bicyclists are not permitted on the trail, since wilderness trails are restricted to hikers and equestrians.

As you begin hiking on Meadow Creek Trail, you will almost immediately cross Meadow Creek, where you can let your pet enjoy the water. Take this trail for 0.8 mile to a fork. If Lily Pad Lakes are your destination, turn right and continue for another 0.5 mile to the larger lake. A smaller lake lies to the north. The views are very pretty from the lake toward Dillon Reservoir and the upper Blue River valley. Return the way you came.

Lily Pad Lake is the destination of a short, pleasant hike along the Meadow Creek Trail.

If you are on your way to Eccles Pass, ignore the Lily Pad Lakes turn-off and bear left on the trail. The Meadow Creek Trail rises steeply as it passes through an aspen forest, then levels off once you reach the lodge-pole pine forest.

At timberline, vistas open up in every direction with panoramic views of the Continental Divide to the east and the Tenmile Range to the south-west. Look for cairns here to stay on the trail.

At about 4 miles, you will intersect with the Gore Range Trail. Take this trail a short distance to Eccles Pass, elevation 11,900 feet.

Return the way you came.

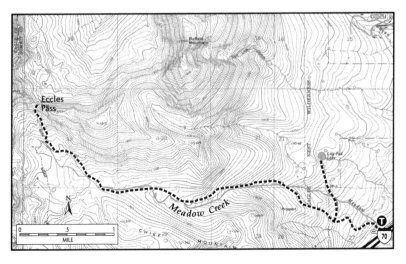

VAIL/COPPER MOUNTAIN

63. Searle Pass

Round trip: 11.4 miles
Hiking time: 10 hours
High point: 12,200 feet
Elevation gain: 2400 feet
Best hiking time: June–October
Maps: USGS Vail Pass; USGS Copper Mountain; Trails Illustrated Vail, Frisco, Dillon (No. 108)
For more information: White River National Forest, Dillon Ranger District, (970) 468-5400

Getting there: From Denver, drive 80 miles west on Interstate 70 to exit 195 at Copper Mountain. Cross the interstate on a bridge and turn right at a paved road in front of the ski resort. Drive past the resort and park in the West Tenmile Creek parking lot. Look for the Colorado Trail (CT) markers.

This is a pleasant hike that explores a broad ascending valley along Guller Creek to Searle Pass. The trail follows the Vail–Copper Mountain bike path for a bit and parallels I-70. The hike offers panoramic views of the Gore Range and the Tenmile Range. This is a very popular cross-country ski destination in the winter.

Start on the bike path and pass under the I-70 overpass. Continue over

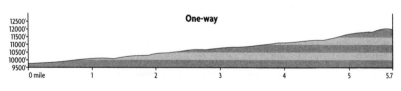

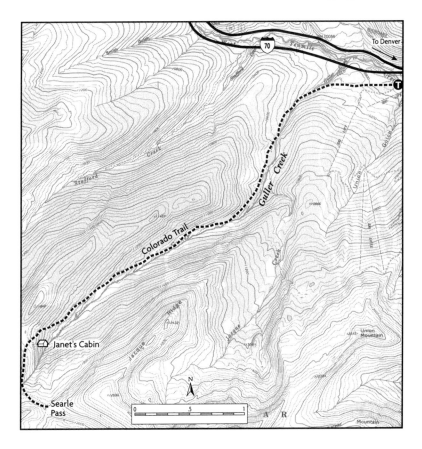

several log-creek crossings before entering the long, wide valley. Guller Creek is nearby, hidden by thick willows, which flame orange in the fall.

The trail climbs a wide meadow up to timberline, but is never that far from a mixed forest. The trees occasionally come closer to create smaller meadows. The ridge to the east is Jacque Ridge. This is one of those hikes that offers tall, wavy grass in which your pet can roll to his heart's content.

However, if you don't want to leave the trail to find water, take plenty of it not only for yourself but also for your dog. If hiking during the height of summer, this trail can get hot.

For a good portion of the hike, you can see your destination, the Searle Pass saddle. It is visible directly south, above timberline. At timberline, you will come across a modern ski lodge, called Janet's Cabin, on your left. The 3000-square-foot hut was completed in 1990 by the Summit Hut

Gore Range vista from Searle Pass

and Trails Association and can sleep up to twenty guests. The hut is named after Janet Boyd Tyler, a Vail resident and avid skier who died in 1988. Space at the hut can be reserved. It is open in winter only.

Continue past the hut. Once you reach the tundra the trail is marked by poles with the CT logo and by cairns. The trail switchbacks and is fairly rocky and steep for the last 0.25 mile.

Admire the views of the Tenmile Range and the Gore Range before turning around. Searle Pass tends to be windy, so if you waited until now to have lunch, descend down the switchbacks before taking your break.

Return the way you came.

64. Wheeler Lakes

Round trip: 4.4 miles
Hiking time: 5 hours
High point: 11,000 feet
Elevation gain: 1300 feet
Best hiking time: June–October
Maps: USGS Vail Pass; Trails Illustrated Vail, Frisco, Dillon (no. 108)
For more information: White River National Forest, Dillon Ranger District, (970) 468-5400

Getting there: From Denver, take Interstate 70 west through the Eisenhower Tunnel. Drive past Frisco to the Copper Mountain ski resort

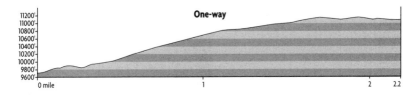

exit (exit 195, Colorado Highway 91). Once on the exit ramp, look sharply to your right for a small pullout for a few cars. The trailhead is on your right just before you cross the bridge over I-70. If the parking area is full, cross the bridge and park at Copper Mountain, then make your way back over the bridge to the trailhead. The trailhead is directly across the interstate from the Copper Mountain tennis courts. There may be a sign that says Uneva Pass/Gore Range Trail.

You will be hiking on the Gore Range Trail, which winds its way through the Eagles Nest Wilderness. The Gore Range, Gore Creek, and other landmarks bearing that name derive from Irish baronet Sir St. George Gore who hunted in the Rockies in the 1850s. The story goes that he traveled in real style and was served meals on fine bone china and drank vintage wine from crystal goblets.

The Gore Range Trail extends north for about 50 miles to south of

View of Copper Mountain ski runs from the turnoff to Wheeler Lakes

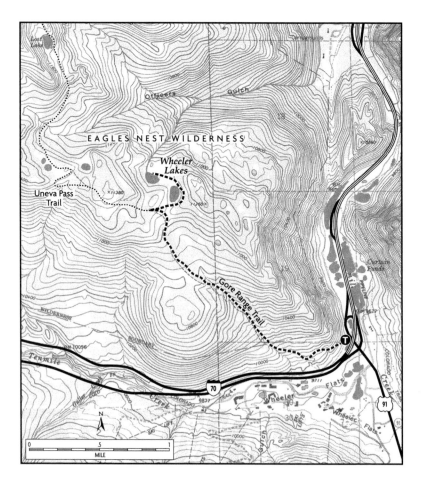

Kremmling. Its southern terminus is at Copper Mountain. This southern section is also known as the Wheeler Trail, which leads to the two charming Wheeler Lakes. The lakes, like the Wheeler Trail and Wheeler Flats (the area around Copper Mountain), are named for John S. Wheeler, who arrived in Colorado in 1859 with other gold prospectors. Eventually he moved to Summit County and established a hay ranch in the meadow that is now Copper Mountain Ski Resort.

Begin hiking northwest from the trailhead. There may be two paths but they merge in a few hundred feet. The ascent is rather steep as you scramble from the notch created by I-70. The trail levels off as it takes you through aspen and pine forest. After 1 mile, there is a Forest Service register nailed to a tree where you can sign in. When you reach a clearing, turn around and enjoy the view of Copper Mountain, Dillon Reservoir, and the Tenmile Range.

At 2 miles, bear right as the trail forks. In another 0.25 mile you will reach the first of the two lakes. The meadow and the lakes offer a lovely spot for some dog frolicking and a picnic lunch. If you have the energy, walk about 0.5 mile past the upper lake to a ridge for a panoramic view of the Continental Divide to the northeast. Uneva Pass (Hike 65) lies 2.5 miles to the northwest, along the main Gore Range Trail.

Return the way you came.

65. Uneva Pass

Round trip: 9 miles
Hiking time: 9–10 hours or backpack
High point: 11,900 feet
Elevation gain: 2200 feet
Best hiking time: June–October
Maps: USGS Vail Pass; Trails Illustrated Vail, Frisco, Dillon (no. 108)
For more information: White River National Forest, Dillon Ranger
District, (970) 468-5400

Getting there: From Denver, take Interstate 70 west through the Eisenhower Tunnel. Drive past Frisco to the Copper Mountain Ski Resort exit (exit 195, Colorado Highway 91). On the exit ramp, look sharply to your right for a small pullout for a few cars. The trailhead is on your right just before you cross the bridge over I-70. If the parking area is full, cross the bridge, then turn left onto a road by the gas station. Continue past the gas station to the Wheeler Flats Recreational Trail parking lot. Hikers on the Copper Mountain–Tennessee Pass segment of the Colorado Trail also use this lot. Carefully make your way back to the west side of I-70 by walking over the bridge. To avoid crossing Colorado Highway 91, you can also park in Copper Mountain Ski Resort. The trailhead is directly across the interstate from the Copper Mountain tennis courts. There may be a sign that says Uneva Pass/Gore Range Trail.

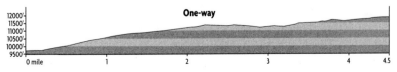

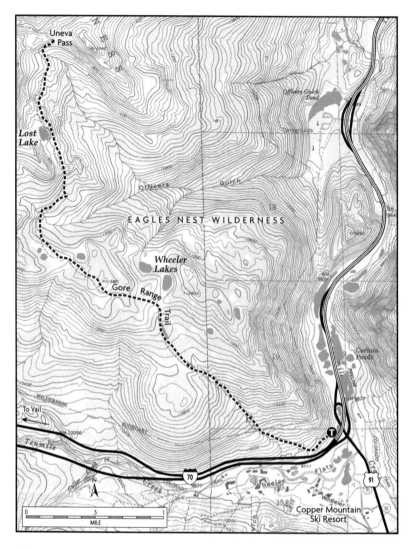

The Gore Range is named after the Irish baronet Sir St. George Gore, who hunted in the Rockies between 1854 and 1857 and explored the range of mountains that today bears his name. He reportedly killed 2000 buffalo in nearby Middle Park and hundreds of other animals.

Gore Range is famous for its sharp ridges and the solitude its rugged terrain offers. The centerpiece of this area is the Eagles Nest Wilderness, where leash regulations for your dog apply. The Gore Range Trail leads north into the wilderness and the terrain ranges from easy to difficult.

As the trail continues north, it intersects with numerous other trails.

From the trailhead, scramble up the slope and pick up the trail, which is clearly visible. Sign in at the Forest Service register after 1 mile. Hike through a forest with intermittent small meadows that offer glimpses of Copper Mountain and the Tenmile Range the higher you climb.

After 2 miles, a spur to the right leads to Wheeler Lakes (Hike 64). Make the 0.5-mile-roundtrip detour, if you wish, then return to the Gore Range Trail. Begin climbing more steeply through an aspen and lodge-pole pine forest for 2 more miles to Lost Lake on your left. Here, both you and your dog can enjoy a well-deserved rest and some fun on the lakeshore.

After the rest continue for about 1 mile to Uneva Pass, elevation 11,900 feet. Watch the weather as you climb above timberline. At the pass, savor vistas of the ski slopes to the south, of the Tenmile Range to the southeast, and of the Continental Divide to the east. The peak to the west is Uneva Peak (12,522 feet). Return the way you came.

Backpacking: The Gore Range Trail provides excellent access to the interior of the rugged and very beautiful Gore Range. It extends for nearly 50 miles from its southern trailhead at Copper Mountain. As the trail travels north, it climbs over Uneva Pass and skirts Uneva Peak to the west.

Uneva Pass on the Gore Range Trail

It continues north to Eccles Pass (Hike 62). From there it passes Cataract Lake, off Colorado Highway 9, 16 miles north of Silverthorne, and ends at Mahan Lake, 15 miles south of Kremmling. The distance between Uneva and Eccles Passes is 8.3 miles. See Hike 62 to develop an interesting backpack loop.

66. Pitkin Lake

Round trip: 8.8 miles
Hiking time: 7 hours
High point: 11,350 feet
Elevation gain: 2900 feet
Best hiking time: July–August
Maps: USGS Vail East; Trails Illustrated Vail, Frisco, Dillon (no. 108)
For more information: White River National Forest, Holy Cross
    Ranger District, (970) 827-5715

Getting there: Take Interstate 70 from Denver west to exit 180/East Vail. Take the exit ramp, then turn sharply right. Drive east less than 0.5 mile, cross Pitkin Creek, and park in the designated spaces for the trailhead, which is next to a condominium complex. The trailhead is on the north side of the North Frontage Road.

Pitkin Creek and Pitkin Lake are named for Frederick W. Pitkin, governor of Colorado from 1879 to 1883. The Pitkin Creek drainage is a narrow, steeply rising glacial bowl that ends in Pitkin Lake with its memorable backdrop of jagged Gore Range peaks. These mountains have not been fully explored by mountaineers to this day. Isolated, seldom-visited valleys lie among the peaks. The Pitkin Lake Trail penetrates this imposing and visually beautiful range. Perhaps because of the paucity of explorers, these peaks have few written descriptions and their names are letters of the alphabet.

    Your canine companion will enjoy this strenuous-yet-satisfying hike because of the continuous presence of clear, gurgling Pitkin Creek, the shaded

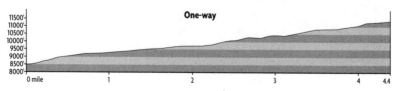

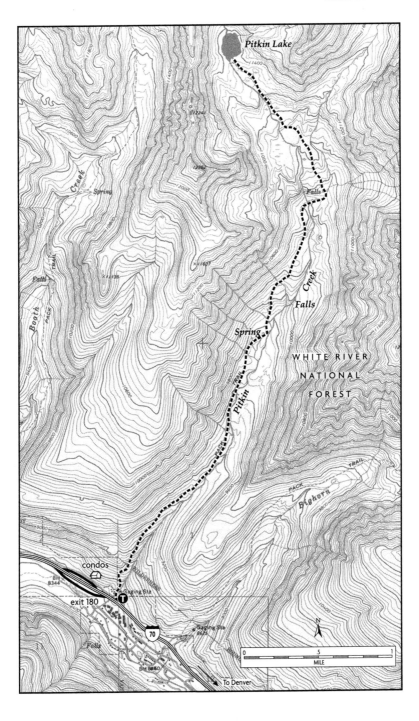

trail, and meadows where there is plenty of room to romp and roll among the summer grasses and wildflowers. And, of course, at the end lies the lake—frigid, but nonetheless begging for a quick swim by an active canine. Pitkin Lake lies in the Eagles Nest Wilderness and leash laws apply.

Sign in at the trail register by the trailhead and cross Pitkin Creek to begin climbing steeply through an aspen grove and past the condominiums. The uphill continues on switchbacks for 1 mile and the narrow trail is well defined and well marked, since the lake is a popular and visually memorable destination.

The terrain levels off as the trail passes through several meadows and the aspen yield to pine. Pitkin Creek tumbles downward nearby, to the west of the trail, always a tempting detour for a swim or a wallow by your dog. The first of five stream crossings is at 1.5 miles.

The rocky trail to Pitkin Lake

At 2.1 miles look for a spring on the left that creates a soft, moist area most dogs adore. It is probably redolent of scents of other wildlife that may also have been drawn to the seeping water and the verdant vegetation surrounding it.

A little over 3 miles into the hike look and listen for the first of the cascades to the right (east) of the trail. The roar of falling water is unmistakable as the trail winds past. Watch your step here and also keep your dog close by since the trail and rocks may be wet and slippery from the overspray.

Continue up through the conifer forest that gives way to smaller meadows and shorter grasses as the valley narrows and elevation increases. Next, gear up for the final ascent to a rocky shelf, then across more level terrain, and up again less steeply to the lake.

The lake is on a rocky flat at the head of the valley. It is a rugged, rocky landscape with little vegetation and some bent old trees. The shoreline consists of small broken rock. On a summer afternoon the sun-warmed rocks invite you to sit down, absorb the vistas, have a snack, and share it with your dog. Return the way you came.

Backpacking: Gore Range is not well hiked, perhaps because of its rugged terrain. Technical skill is needed to summit many of its peaks. Camping is possible on the shelf near Pitkin Lake. Going farther will require careful preparation, but will offer uncommon solitude. A Gore Range backpack is primarily for the advanced hiker.

67. Booth Falls and Booth Lake

Round trip: 8 miles
Hiking time: 7 hours
High point: 11,500 feet
Elevation gain: 3050 feet
Best hiking time: July–August
Maps: USGS Vail East; Trails Illustrated Vail, Frisco, Dillon (no. 108)
For more information: White River National Forest, Holy Cross
   Ranger District, (970) 827-5715

Getting there: Take Interstate 70 from Denver west to exit 180/East Vail. Turn north and almost immediately left onto the North Frontage Road and drive 0.7 mile west to the turnoff for Booth Falls Road. Turn right (north) and pass the Vail Mountain School and its overflow parking lot. Continue another 0.2 mile to the parking lot at the trailhead.

Visitors to Vail, as well as locals, hike up to Booth Falls because the 60-foot waterfall is lovely and the general belief is that the falls are easy to reach. But, believe me, this is no gentle alpine ramble. The hike to the falls is 2 miles one-way with an elevation gain of 1500 feet—not exactly a cakewalk. Moreover, Booth Lake is another 2 miles uphill with an additional elevation gain of another 1500 feet for a total gain of 3000 feet.

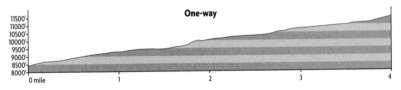

No wonder then that most hikers turn around at the falls. So if you are in fine shape and your dog is trail hardened and used to high altitude, do go to the lake, but be forewarned. This hike is an all-day affair. If you are a fisherman, there is an added bonus: Booth Lake offers good fishing and even has an island.

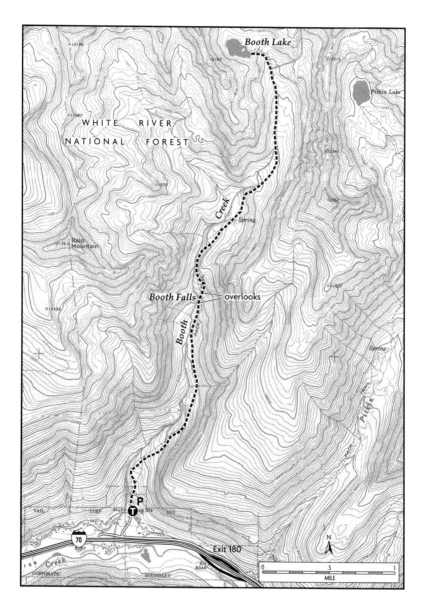

Charlie with Rover at Booth Falls (Photo by Yue Savage)

Rivulets and streamlets crossing the trail to join nearby Booth Creek offer continual hydration and cooling pleasure for your dog. Nonetheless, take plenty of water along and make sure you and your dog are adequately hydrated, especially if you are hiking on a hot summer day.

Start at the gate at the north end of the parking lot. Walk up the gravel road to a trail sign and a register. Enter a grove of aspen and start climbing on a narrow dirt trail. What makes the hike challenging is that you are given no opportunity to raise your heart rate slowly and steadily. The trail starts off steeply right at the trailhead. The positive aspect of this stretch is that it is in dappled shade and you cross to the other side of the creek, so your dog has a chance to get some water.

After 0.3 mile of switchbacks, the terrain becomes more gradual and vistas open up to the southwest with good views of the Vail valley and the ribbon of I-70.

Beyond a grove of Colorado blue spruce, the trail widens so that you and your canine companion can walk side by side. But then comes rocky terrain and an uphill push that should be negotiated with care.

At 1 mile, rock-strewn Booth Creek joins the trail and offers the opportunity for you to rest and for your dog to enjoy the clear, tumbling water. The nearby meadow is covered with midseason blooming scarlet fireweed and other wildflowers.

The trail then levels and drops a little to a small stream crossing before continuing uphill again to another stream crossing—nirvana for any dog who is working hard. A pleasant copse of aspen and thimbleberries offers interesting scents for your dog of the wildlife that uses the plentiful vegetation as shelter and habitat. Pause here to watch your dog sniff and follow his gaze. This may help you catch a glimpse of one of these critters.

Switchbacks take you higher to just below the falls. At 1.8 miles from the trailhead, cross a small talus field. Keep close watch on your dog here since loose rocks that are disturbed can be sent hurtling downward. Make certain your dog stays on the trail next to you. The next uphill grind takes you to the bottom of the falls.

Here the trail divides. Go left a few hundred feet to a spectacular overlook of the lower falls. There is a swimming hole at the base of the lower falls that both you and your dog can enjoy. The water is frigid, I am told.

After absorbing the vista, return to the main trail and continue to the falls. After another 0.2 mile the crash of falling water tells you that the waterfall is near. Take another fork left. It leads to the edge of the gorge and a view of the waterfall. It is best to keep your dog close to you in this area, since the rocks are slippery and hang out over the gorge.

Continuing beyond the falls, early-season hikers may encounter small snowfields on the trail where rock outcrops cast shadows across the ground. Stands of trees alternate with several meadows filled with seasonal wildflowers. Look for the abundant columbine, paintbrush, and larkspur in these meadows.

Above 10,000 feet, trees thin out to offer views of the serrated ridges of the Gore Range. At 2.5 miles from the trailhead there is a junction with the Upper Piney Creek Trail. Keep right here.

At 3 miles, cross a side creek of Booth Creek and continue north for another 1 mile to Booth Lake. If you encounter some serious hikers that are going beyond the lake, they may be heading for East Partner Peak, which at 13,041 feet has made it onto the Thirteener list. Return the way you came.

Backpacking: You can camp at Booth Lake, but you must camp at least 100 feet away from the edge of the lake. Please use Leave No Trace camping techniques to minimize the high use of this area.

LEADVILLE/ BUENA VISTA

68. Kroenke Lake

Round trip: 8 miles
Hiking time: 7 hours
High point: 11,530 feet
Elevation gain: 1700 feet
Best hiking time: July–August
Maps: USGS Mount Yale; Trails Illustrated Buena Vista (no. 129)
For more information: San Isabel National Forest, Salida Ranger
District, (719) 539-3591

Getting there: From the traffic light in Buena Vista off U.S. Highway 24 and Main Street, go north 0.4 mile to Crossman Avenue (County Road 350). Turn left and drive west 1.5 miles until the road dead-ends in County Road 361. Turn right (north) and continue on County Road 361 for 0.9 mile. Make a sharp left turn onto County Road 365, which is unpaved. This road is also known as North Cottonwood Creek Road and a Forest Service sign may indicate this. This road jogs south 0.2 mile before turning west and continuing for 5 miles to its end at the North Cottonwood Creek Trail trailhead. There are ample parking spaces and several campsites nearby.

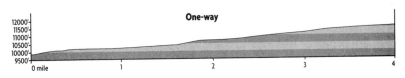

One-way

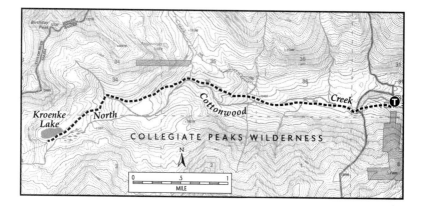

This hike follows a tumbling stream and travels through a mountain forest to end at Kroenke Lake. The hike is in the Collegiate Peaks Wilderness so wilderness leash regulations apply. Nonetheless, the hike meets the two criteria that make an outing a joy for any dog—plenty of water access and a trail that is not hard on paws.

From the trailhead, the North Cottonwood Creek Trail runs along the creek for about 50 yards before crossing it on a solid bridge. The trail follows the stream, offering numerous opportunities for your dog to get wet or get a drink. The trail passes through a dense mixed forest and at 1.5 miles crosses the stream again.

Just past the crossing, the trail splits. Bear left (west) on the Kroenke Lake Trail that leads to the lake and Browns Pass on the Continental Divide.

Kroenke Lake lies 2.5 miles ahead at the base of the Continental Divide. The trail steepens as it climbs to the lake. Two more stream crossings are pleasant experiences for your dog. The terrain dips before reaching the lake. The shelf around the lake is covered with evergreens and meadows. Notice the tiny island almost in the center of the lake.

On a beautiful Colorado afternoon, a lakeside lunch offers dramatic vistas of the Continental Divide to the west and the summit of Mount Yale (14,196 feet) to the southeast.

Return the way you came.

Backpacking: An interesting backpack in this area is in the Horn Fork Basin. To reach this basin, take the right fork 1 mile from the trailhead and follow the trail into the basin. The trail is the south access trail to Mount Harvard (14,420 feet). Or after reaching Kroenke Lake, hike up to Browns Pass and the Continental Divide Trail.

69. Waterdog Lakes

Round trip: 3.6 miles
Hiking time: 4 hours
High point: 11,400 feet
Elevation gain: 1000 feet
Best hiking time: July–mid-September
Maps: USGS Garfield; Trails Illustrated Salida, St. Elmo, Shavano
  Peak (no. 130)
For more information: San Isabel National Forest, Salida Ranger
  District, (719) 539-3591

Getting there: From Poncha Springs take U.S. Highway 50. Drive west, traveling toward Monarch Pass. In approximately 13.5 miles, pass the Monarch Mountain Lodge located on the left side of the highway. Continue traveling for 2.5 miles. The parking area is a small highway pullout

Easy uphill trail to Waterdog Lakes

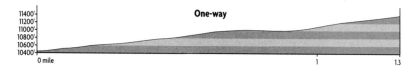

located on the left side of the road. The trailhead is located on the opposite side of the highway and is difficult to see at highway speed. A small brown sign marks the start of the trail.

If you and your dog are constant hiking and backpacking companions, then a quick day trip or an easy overnight backpack to Waterdog Lakes may be fun. The trail is easy to reach and the hike elevation is modest.

The scant 2-mile-long trail follows a stream as it winds its way upward through an evergreen forest. In the meadows and clearings, wildflowers are abundant during July and August. The lakes are at timberline and beneath the rock wall of the Continental Divide.

The maintained trail ends at the lower lake. To reach the upper lake, look for a fisherman's trail leading in a northeasterly direction. The upper lake is great for brook trout.

Backpacking: Camping is permitted 100 feet from the lakeshores.

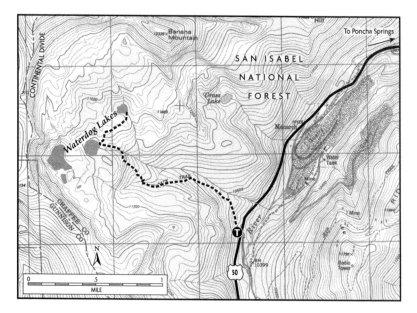

ASPEN/ BASALT

70. Lost Man Trail Loop

Half loop: 8.5 miles
Hiking time: 7 hours
High point: 12,800 feet
Elevation gain: 1300 feet
Best hiking time: Late July–August
Maps: USGS Mount Champion; USGS Thimble Rock; Trails Illustrated Aspen, Independence Pass (no. 127)
For more information: White River National Forest, Aspen Ranger District, (970) 925-3445.

Getting there: From Aspen, drive 14 miles east on Colorado Highway 82 toward Independence Pass to the parking lot directly across from Lost Man Campground. The campground, with drinking water and toilets, is directly across the highway from the trailhead, which is on the left (north) side of the highway. Leave one car here for a shuttle.

Continue with another vehicle 4 miles more to the last switchback before the top of Independence Pass. Park on the left (north) side of the road.

This hike, in the Hunter-Fryingpan Wilderness where leash laws apply, offers you and your canine companion three options, depending on your and your dog's hiking abilities, stamina, available time, and weather. The first option is a short hike to Linkins Lake, situated above timberline and

just below the summit of Independence Pass. The second option is to continue along Lost Man Creek to Independence Lake, another gorgeous alpine lake, but one offering more solitude than Linkins Lake.

If the weather and your and your dog's stamina hold, you may want to consider option three. It continues to the saddle above Independence Lake, the highest point on this trail, for superb views of the Continental Divide and the Roaring Fork River valley. Then complete a half loop back to Lost Man Campground.

Another fun thing to do in this area is to take a guided hike. The Aspen Center for Environmental Studies at Hallam Lake conducts hikes with naturalists on trails such as Lost Man Trail. See Appendix A for the group's contact information.

For any option, starting at the Linkins Lake end enables you to be above timberline early in the day, so the chance of being caught in a

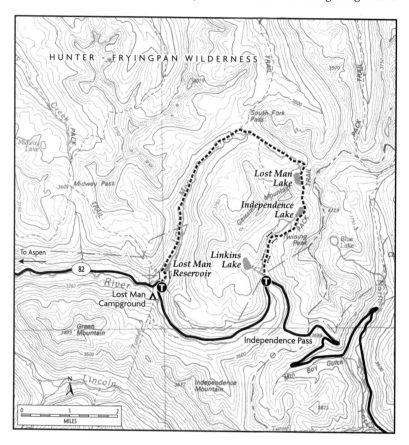

Looking down into Fryingpan drainage

sudden afternoon thunderstorm above timberline on this hike is less probable. Be aware that you will be hiking at a very lofty altitude, so use plenty of sunscreen, take along plenty of water, and layer your clothing. Watch your dog for signs of fatigue, which may result from high-altitude hiking. Make certain he is very well hydrated and stop if he starts lagging behind or loses his customary pep.

One final note is that snow tends to linger on the trail into July and sections of the trail may be very muddy early in the season, if not snow covered. Look for marsh marigolds in the wetter, boggier places.

You will have one tired-but-happy dog after this hike. Most of the hike is on soft tundra and the sources to water are truly innumerable, since you will be hiking not only past three lakes but also along two creek drainages.

Begin hiking from the Linkins Lake trailhead. Both the Linkins Lake Trail and the Lost Man Trail ascend together a short distance and cross a stream, one of numerous such stream crossings along the way. At the Hunter-Fryingpan Wilderness sign, the Lost Man Trail continues right (north), while the Linkins Lake Trail bends left (west) to begin a steep climb to the shelf on which the lake rests. The trail levels off as it crosses the tundra to the lake. The distance to the lake is 0.5 mile one-way.

If you continue on the Lost Man Trail, you will hike along the Roaring Fork River for 0.3 mile before crossing to the other side. This starts the climb upward as the trail rises to a plateau above the bowl. At about 2 miles from the trailhead, the trail crosses the river once again over rocky terrain as you head for Independence Lake at 12,490 feet and 2.1 miles from the trailhead.

By now your dog will have gotten wet and most likely muddy if you are hiking in early season. Make certain that the high-pitched cry of the pica, a small animal that resides in the tundra, does not send your dog off the trail. Conserve his and your strength.

Independence Lake is a great place for a break. The Continental Divide is the huge rock wall to your right (east). The mountain across to the west is Geissler Mountain with east and west summits, 13,200 and 13,301 feet respectively.

From the lake, follow the trail along the shoreline and climb steeply to the saddle between the Roaring Fork and Lost Man Creek drainages. This is Lost Man Pass, elevation 12,800 feet, the high point of the hike. The trail leading to the pass snakes through a talus field. Follow the cairns and make sure your dog stays on the trail for his safety.

Lost Man Lake is some 400 feet below, surrounded by impressive boulders. Once you drop to the lake, you may want to take another breather and give your dog a chance to enjoy the water.

Next, pass Lost Man Lake along its right (east) shore and continue on the trail as it swings west in a big curve to cross the outlet stream and descend farther into the Lost Man Creek drainage. Stay on the Lost Man Trail. Don't be tempted by the faint trail going off to the left (south). The Forest Service does not maintain it and it climbs the saddle between the two peaks of Geissler Mountain before reaching the highway. The climb is extremely steep.

Continue on the Lost Man Trail to a signed T junction and stay to the left (the right goes to South Fork Pass). Stay on the Lost Man Trail as it continues its descent to timberline and Lost Man Creek. Hike on the west side of the creek past waterfalls and stepped cascades. Continue downhill into a large meadow. Lost Man Reservoir lies at the far end. This is the last chance for your dog to swim and engage in a game of fetch in the water.

Stay on the trail along the west shore of the reservoir. At this point you are a mere 0.5 mile from the end of the hike. Stay straight ahead when you come to the Midway Pass Trail spur and cross a wooden bridge. The trail ends to the right of the Forest Service bulletin board.

Backpacking: The Hunter-Fryingpan Wilderness consists of 74,000 acres of high peaks and precipitous valleys. A possible backpack takes you across South Fork Pass and into Deadman Gulch. Make sure to take sufficient gear for a sudden cold spell, possible even in the summer.

71. Maroon Lake, Crater Lake, and Buckskin Pass

Round trip: 8.5 miles
Hiking time: 7 hours
High point: 12,733 feet
Elevation gain: 3150 feet
Best hiking time: July–August
Maps: USGS Maroon Bells; Trails Illustrated Maroon Bells, Redstone, Marble (no. 128)
For more information: White River National Forest, Aspen Ranger District, (970) 925-3445

Getting there: Drive west from Aspen on Colorado Highway 82 to Maroon Creek Road. There is a traffic light and a chapel at the intersection. Turn left and bear right immediately at the fork in the road. Continue on Maroon Creek Road for 9.6 miles to Maroon Lake and the adjacent parking lot, where there are toilets, picnic facilities, and information available.

There is a shuttle bus from Aspen from mid-May through mid-September that you must take if you are setting out after 8:30 AM, which is when the Maroon Lake Road closes to private cars. Shuttle stops are near the McDonald's in town or at the Highlands Ski Area off Colorado Highway 82. People pay a fee, but dogs ride free. Call the ranger district for information.

When you are in Aspen, you must see the Maroon Bells, the most deadly and arguably the most beautiful and most photographed mountains in Colorado. You will not be alone in this sightseeing endeavor, so preplanning is necessary. In peak season, either plan an early start, or plan on taking the shuttle bus from Aspen.

So there are a lot of people at Maroon Lake, whose surface reflects the uneven striations of North Maroon Peak and Maroon Peak, the Maroon Bells. The meadow beyond the parking lot is a great place to take in this incredible view, but if you and your canine companion crave a bit of solitude and

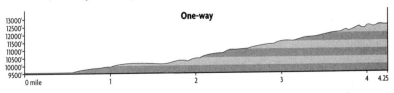

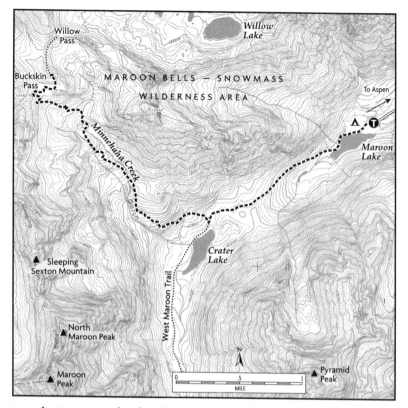

a workout, you need to head out and away. Most visitors follow the spa-ghetti-like web of trails around the lake or opt for the Maroon Creek Trail that heads through meadows and back down the access road.

This hike travels past Maroon Lake to Crater Lake and then up some steep-but-manageable pitches to a beautiful basin surrounded by breath-taking peaks, and then on to Buckskin Pass. You will meet hikers on this trail—especially on a sunny weekend—but their numbers will be substan-tially fewer than on the trails in the basin below. The hike is in the Ma-roon Bells–Snowmass Wilderness Area and leash regulations apply.

Leaving the parking lot, keep to the far right side and walk through the meadow that undulates with wildflowers and through a small aspen grove in the direction of Maroon Lake. At an intersection, pick up the signed Maroon-Snowmass Trail and head southwest. Pass a sign that warns visitors about the dangers of climbing the Maroon Bells. Continue along the north side of Maroon Lake and pass another sign, this one at the wilderness boundary.

The trail ascends as you make your way over exposed tree roots and past medium-sized rocks from an old rock slide. Continue on the Maroon-Snowmass Trail at all intersections and head toward Crater Lake, climbing vigorously up a headwall to the shelf where the lake lies. Crater Lake will come into view on your left. Just short of the lake, at 1.6 miles, the Maroon-Snowmass Trail veers off to the right (northwest). Stay on this trail if you are going to Buckskin Pass.

If you would rather cut the hike short, take the West Maroon Trail to Crater Lake, which offers superb views of the Bells and of Pyramid Peak, all Fourteeners that are members of what are locally called "The Dirty Dozen"— Fourteeners built of crumbling, rotten rock that can give way underfoot at any moment. Annually there is a major accident or fatality on the Bells.

From Crater Lake retrace your steps to the Maroon-Snowmass Trail, turn right and return to the parking lot. Climbing on the Maroon-Snowmass Trail to Buckskin Pass is strenuous and gives you a taste of hiking in the Elk Range. After several switchbacks, the trail levels off as it enters a park-like basin of meadows and tree copses.

The trail follows Minnehaha Creek in the shade of aspen groves and spruce stands, which your dog will appreciate. Wet spots and rivulets along the trail are other sources of pleasure for your pet. When you come to a small stream that flows into the creek, you may want to pause so your pet can get his fill of water and cool down if it is a hot morning. In the meadows you pass, look for carpets of red king's crown during summer's peak. Also stop and look southeast to Crater Lake. Beyond it rises imposing Pyramid Peak, creating a memorable vista.

The mountains to your left (west) are the Bells. The mountain to their right is Sleeping Sexton. In

North Maroon rises above trail to Buckskin Pass. (Photo by Jim Gehres)

another 0.4 mile you get a glimpse of Buckskin Pass, the dip in the ridge to the northwest. Pass through a meadow with signs noting that camping is prohibited in this area. When you come to a trail junction at the far side of the meadow, bear left. (The right fork goes to Willow Pass and Willow Lake, good backpacking destinations.)

Here, above timberline, the valley splits. The whistles that make your dog stop and prick his ears are coming from roly-poly marmots as they keep watch above their burrows. Keep an eye on your dog so he does not try to leave the trail to investigate these shrill whistles or the yelps of the fast-moving pica.

As you approach the final segment to Buckskin Pass you may encounter remnants of a large snowfield that lingers here far into the summer. This last segment of the hike is the hardest as you gain 700 feet in elevation in the final 1 mile on tough, tight switchbacks.

The pass offers spectacular 360-degree views of the Elk Range. West of the pass, Snowmass Mountain (14,092 feet) rises into the sky. Hagerman Peak is to the left of Snowmass and Capitol Peak is farthest to the north. A sawtooth ridge extends from Buckskin Pass south to North Maroon Peak. Return the way you came.

Backpacking: A trail descends to Snowmass Lake, a hard climb back up but a great backpacking destination. Willow Pass and Willow Lake are other tempting destinations.

72. Hardscrabble and Williams Lakes

Round trip: 4 miles
Hiking time: 4 hours
High point: 10,815 feet
Elevation gain: 1300 feet
Best hiking time: July–August
Maps: USGS Capitol Peak; Trails Illustrated Maroon Bells, Redstone, Marble (no. 128)
For more information: White River National Forest, Aspen Ranger District, (970) 925-3445

Getting there: To access the trailhead, a high-clearance vehicle is necessary. Take Colorado Highway 82 northwest from Aspen for 14 miles

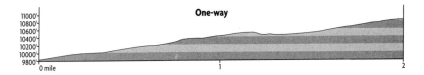

to Old Snowmass. The turnoff is about 4 miles south of the Basalt Bypass. Turn left (west) onto Snowmass Road. Continue for 1.8 miles to a T junction and turn right (west) onto the Capitol Creek Road. The pavement ends at 6.4 miles from the Highway 82 turnoff. The road becomes rough at 9 miles. Continue past the Capitol Creek Trail trailhead. The Williams Lake trailhead is another 1.5 miles up the very rough road and only high-clearance vehicles can make it that far.

The jostling ride to the trailhead is worthwhile just for the scenery. The hike itself offers a closer look at the north side of the Elk Range and of Capitol Peak (14,130 feet), one of the hardest to climb and most beautiful of the Fourteeners. This trip to two lakes also gets you to water, a treat for your canine companion while you ogle the scenery.

Do bring mosquito repellent, and leash laws apply because you will be hiking in the Maroon Bells–Snowmass Wilderness Area.

As you start down the trail, the exposed slopes of Capitol Peak dominate the view. Pass the green gate at the Williams Lake trailhead and continue through a stand of aspen. Pass a wilderness boundary sign and

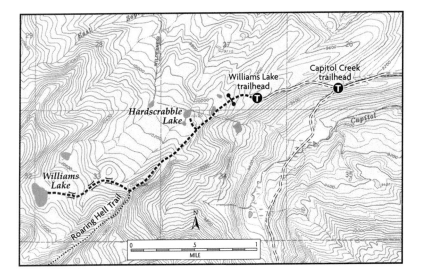

Capitol Peak dominates the skyline. (Photo by Jim Gehres)

watch your step as exposed tree roots crisscross the trail. You might want to stop at the small pond on your right for your dog to get his feet wet and lap some water.

Climb uphill and stay to your left to avoid a social trail that peters out. Continue through the mature spruce and fir forest and look for the turnoff for Hardscrabble Lake in a short 0.5 mile from the trailhead. There should be a sign pointing to your right (north). The lake is just a few hundred yards north of the main trail, up to the shelf. The lake is oval in shape, much smaller than Williams Lake and an unusual emerald green in color.

Return to the main trail, turn right (west), and start hiking uphill. At 1.5 miles from the trailhead the Roaring Hell Trail veers to the left (southwest) at the base of a short downhill pitch. Continue straight ahead, climbing uphill and down as the trail stretches upward to the forested ridgeline.

Pass through a boggy area where mosquitoes can be fierce. Here boardwalks and a series of bridges take you over the wetter spots and several creeks. Follow one of these creeks, with several cascades, up to the shelf where Williams Lake lies, surrounded by boulders and evergreen trees.

Sitting on one of the sun-warmed boulders and savoring the solitude and peace, while your dog lies at your feet, it is hard to imagine why and how Hardscrabble Lake got its name or, for the matter, how Roaring Hell Trail was named. Return the way you came.

Backpacking: The Maroon Bells–Snowmass Wilderness consists of 74,000 acres with extensive trail systems. Since 2003 free permits are required to camp in the wilderness. A recommended backpack is in Conundrum Creek drainage on the western slope of Capitol Peak.

SAN JUAN MOUNTAINS

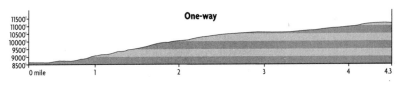

73. Waterdog Lake

Round trip: 8.6 miles
Hiking time: 6–7 hours
High point: 11,100 feet
Elevation gain: 2500 feet
Best hiking time: Mid-June–October
Maps: USGS Lake City; Trail Illustrated Telluride, Silverton, Ouray, Lake City (no. 141)
For more information: Bureau of Land Management, Gunnison Field Office, (970) 641-0471

Getting there: From Colorado Highway 149, cross the bridge over the Lake Fork of the Gunnison River at the north end of Lake City. Turn left and walk one block. Turn left again to the sewage treatment plant. If driving, park next to the plant's fence in the trailhead area that is signed. From the sewage treatment plant, walk along the road for 0.25 mile to the first house you see. As you reach it look for a sign on the right that indicates the trailhead to the lake trail.

Camping is permitted at Waterdog Lake.

What a hike! You don't need to drive if you are already in Lake City. Best of all, your dog will love it. The hike is on Bureau of Land Management

(BLM) land, so your pet can be off-leash. Since the trail winds through a forest, there is plenty of shade and water along the way.

This hike was discovered through what turned out to be a fortuitous turn of events. Being stuck in Lake City because of car trouble we fretted that our hiking plans had to be canceled. A local resident who overheard us talking about our troubles suggested that we explore "Waterdog Reservoir" close to town. So we did while the car was being fixed.

Since it starts close to town, the trail passes through private property for the first 0.25 mile. Keep your dog on a leash and stay on the trail. The

trail is clearly posted, as is the private land. Once the trail ascends the hill ahead of you, it reaches public land. This is near a powerline.

Once you reach the hilltop, pause and turn around to savor a pretty vista of Lake City. For the next mile, your canine companion can enjoy off-leash freedom. Pass through a lovely stand of aspen. It was aglow with molten gold on our hike. At 2 miles from the trailhead, the trail reaches the northern boundary of Horse Park, privately owned and barred to hikers. At this point, follow the sign to turn left (northeast) sharply and continue through the aspen forest for another 1 mile. Most of this terrain is privately owned so your dog should be on the leash until BLM property is reached again.

Cross Park Creek at 3 miles from the trailhead and enter BLM land. A short distance before the lake, the trail joins a jeep road. Turn left (north) and follow the road to Waterdog Lake. Return the way you came.

Waterdog Lake Trail near Lake City

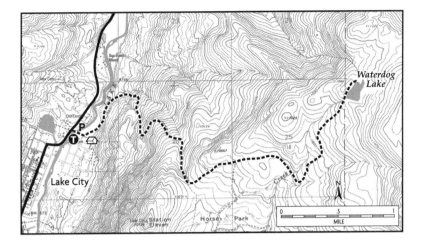

74. American Basin

Round trip: 4 miles
Hiking time: 3 hours
High point: 12,950 feet
Elevation gain: 1650 feet
Best hiking time: Mid-July–mid-August
Maps: USGS Handies Peak; USGS Redcloud Peak; Trails Illustrated
Telluride, Silverton, Ouray, Lake City (no. 141)
For more information: Bureau of Land Management, Gunnison Field
Office, (970) 641-0471

Getting there: A high-clearance vehicle is needed to reach the trailhead.
From Lake City, take Colorado Highway 149 south 2.5 miles. Turn right
onto the road to Lake San Cristobal. Follow the paved road about 4 miles,
then continue on dirt road for 16.3 miles. The American Basin road
begins at a fork where a sign reads "Cinnamon Pass/American Basin."
Take the left fork. Drive 1.75 miles to the trailhead. Parking and camping is available near the trailhead.

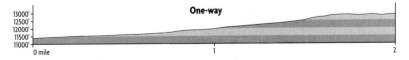

American Basin can be easily reached from Lake City but it is lightly hiked even though at the height of the summer the basin is spectacular with wildflowers and is one of the most beautiful areas of the San Juan Mountains. Your dog will love the soft grass, the rolling meadows, and access to a refreshing dip in Sloan Lake at the end of the trail. Sloan Lake is the habitat of the threatened Colorado cutthroat trout. Since this hike is on Bureau of Land Management land, dogs can be off-leash.

The hike is at and above timberline. The trail ascends through an incredible meadow abloom with a riot of flowers, some reaching knee-high with their nodding heads. The trail traverses the lower west flank of Handies Peak (14,048 feet, Hike 80). Reach Sloan Lake in 2 miles and

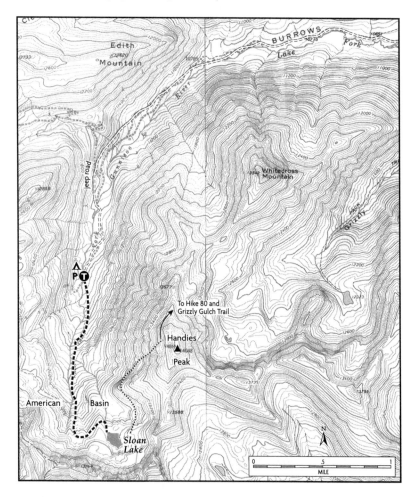

Handies Peak towers over American Basin. (Photo by Jim Gehres)

enjoy the wide open vistas to the south and west. More ambitious hikers may pass you at Sloan Lake. They are using the alternate route to
reach this easy Fourteener's summit.

You can combine the American Basin Trail with the Grizzly Gulch Trail
that climbs Handies Peak to make a loop trip (see Hike 80). For a downhill hike at the end of the day, begin at the Grizzly Gulch trailhead, hike
up to Handies Peak and then down through American Basin to the main
road and back to the Grizzly Gulch trailhead. This is a 10-mile loop. Avoid
hiking the access road between trailheads by arranging for a car shuttle.

GRAND JUNCTION

75. Water Dog Reservoir to Twin Basin Reservoir

Round trip: 7.3 miles
Hiking time: 5 hours
High point: 9990 feet
Elevation gain: 350 feet
Best hiking time: May–October
Maps: USGS Grand Mesa; Trails Illustrated Grand Mesa (no. 136); trail map available at the Grand Mesa Visitor Center
For more information: Grand Mesa National Forest, Grand Valley Ranger District, (970) 242-8211 or (970) 856-4153

Getting there: From Interstate 70 about 17 miles east of Grand Junction, take exit 49/Mesa/Colorado Highway 65/Grand Mesa Scenic Byway, right (east). Continue on Highway 65 past the town of Mesa where the highway turns south. Travel to Powderhorn Ski Area on a winding and scenic road. Once past Powderhorn, continue 5 miles to the turnoff for Mesa Lakes Lodge and the Jumbo Lake Road. Park at the large parking lot at the intersection.

The Grand Mesa Visitor Center is on top of the Grand Mesa just east of the Colorado Highway 65 on Trickle Park Road, across from Cobbett Lake.

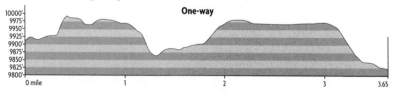

It is open between 9:00 AM and 5:00 PM daily during the summer.

With a name like Water Dog Reservoir—well, what more needs to be said? This is a flat trail that runs northeast along what was once a farm road. The trail passes five reservoirs, lakes, and beaver ponds and is typical of the hiking experience on Grand Mesa—a lot of water for fishing, swimming, and water skiing. The terrain alternates from aspen groves to a fir and spruce forest to clearings and meadows. At higher elevation, the ecosystem becomes drier and more barren with piñon pine and sagebrush flanking the trails.

Your dog will enjoy the multiple opportunities for swimming and romping in the water. (And bring mosquito repellent, since parts of the trail are marshy.) Although your dog has to be on a leash on the trail, it is okay to take the leash off at the water's edge to let him go swimming or to play a game of fetch. Once on land, the leash must be reattached.

From the east end of the parking lot, take the Water Dog Reservoir/ Long Slough Trail. Reach Water Dog Reservoir in 0.25 mile and stop for your canine companion's first dip. Then pass the reservoir and climb a small knoll, the highest point on the hike.

In the next 1 mile pass through aspen groves and scrub oak and skirt

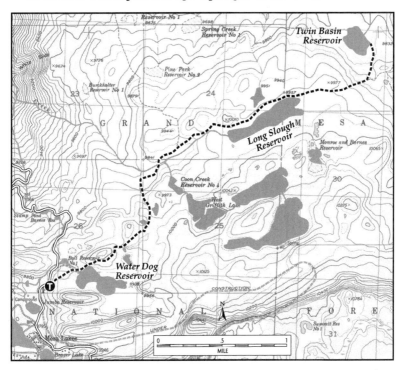

Grand Mesa is dotted with lakes and ponds.

three small ponds. Drop to a marshy area and keep right at a fork at 1.75 miles, then climb gradually uphill to Long Slough Reservoir, a long and narrow body of water just a few hundred feet off the trail to your right. Once the level trail runs the length of the reservoir it comes to its banks and connects with a footpath loop around the lake.

The main trail then swings to the east past the reservoir. Descend 150 feet and bear left (north) at a fork before reaching Twin Basin Reservoir. Return the way you came.

76. Mesa Lakes and Lost Lake

Round trip: 2.2 miles
Hiking time: 1.5 hours
High point: 10,200 feet
Elevation gain: 300 feet
Best hiking time: May–October
Maps: USGS Grand Mesa; Trails Illustrated Grand Mesa (no. 136);
    trail map available at the Grand Mesa Visitor Center
For more information: Grand Mesa National Forest, Grand Valley
    Ranger District, (970) 242-8211 or (970) 856-4153

Getting there: Take Interstate 70 east from Grand Junction for 17 miles to exit 49/ Mesa/Colorado Highway 65/Grand Mesa Scenic Byway. Travel 25 miles south to the Mesa Lakes turnoff, which is about 5 miles past the Powderhorn Ski Area. Drive into the Mesa Lakes Resort and con-

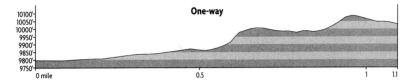

tinue to Sunset Lake. At Sunset Lake turn left (southeast) and park in the picnic area or campground lots. The Grand Mesa Visitor Center is on top of the Grand Mesa just east of the Colorado Highway 65 on Trickle Park Road, across from Cobbett Lake. It is open between 9:00 AM and 5:00 PM daily during the summer.

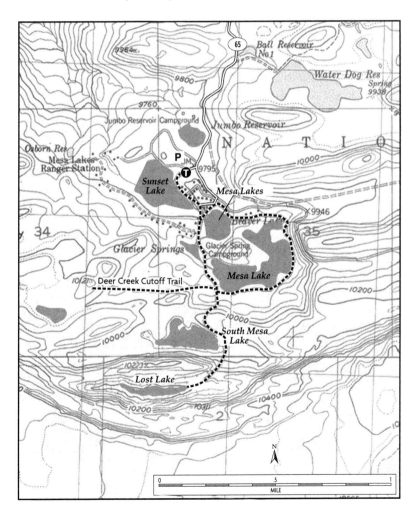

Like many of the hikes on Grand Mesa, this hike has little elevation gain to tax you but it is sheer joy for your canine companion. Grand Mesa is studded with hundreds of lakes, reservoirs, and beaver ponds. Although your dog has to stay on-leash on the trail, at the lake's edge the leash comes off and he can frolic in the water. This hike offers such opportunities at five different lakes, so enjoy. But also bring plenty of mosquito repellent during summer months or after a wet spell in early fall.

After parking your car, hike south from Sunset Lake and pick up the Mesa Lake Shore Trail loop. Take this trail counterclockwise, keeping the lake on your left. The trail passes through stands of evergreens and copses of aspen as it heads south toward a ridgeline.

Pass the junction on your right with the Deer Creek Cutoff Trail and in a short distance pick up the Lost Lake Trail that goes off to the right (southwest). Pass South Mesa Lake on your right and continue south to climb a crest.

Return the way you came or, to make the hike longer, turn right (east) on the Mesa Lake Shore Trail and circle it counterclockwise to your starting point. The counterclockwise loop segment is about 1 mile long.

One of the many lakes you'll see on Grand Mesa

77. Crag Crest National Recreation Trail Loop

Round trip: 8.7-mile loop
Hiking time: 8 hours
High point: 11,150 feet
Elevation gain: 1050 feet
Best hiking time: May–October
Maps: USGS Grand Mesa; Trails Illustrated Grand Mesa (no. 136);
trail map available at the Grand Mesa Visitor Center
For more information: Grand Mesa National Forest, Grand Valley
Ranger District, (970) 242-8211 or (970) 856-4153

Getting there: Take Interstate 70 east from Grand Junction for 17 miles
to exit 49/ Mesa/Colorado Highway 65/Grand Mesa Scenic Byway. Travel
34 miles south to the west trailhead of Crag Crest Trail at the side of
the highway.

The Grand Mesa Visitor Center is on top of the Grand Mesa just east of
the Colorado Highway 65 on Trickle Park Road, across from Cobbett Lake.
It is open between 9:00 AM and 5:00 PM daily during the summer.

The Crag Crest Trail was designated a National Recreation Trail in 1978.
It is a loop consisting of a crest portion and a lower segment and can be
accessed from two trailheads, one on the west end across from Island Lake
and one on the east end adjacent to Eggleston Lake. A car shuttle is an
option if you want to forgo the loop.

If you are a hiker who lives in or is visiting Grand Junction, you have
heard stories about the Crag Crest Trail, its magnificent vistas, and its ver-
tigo drop-offs. The crest segment rises steeply from the east trailhead to
the top of Crag Crest. From the west trailhead, the crest portion rises more
gradually, so a start from the west trailhead is recommended. A 50-yard
segment of the trail is very narrow, about 2 to 3 feet wide with drop-offs
on both sides. Otherwise, the trail is about 20 feet across. If you or your
dog are not sure you can or want to handle that super-narrow segment,

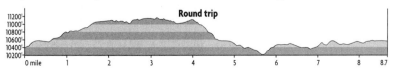

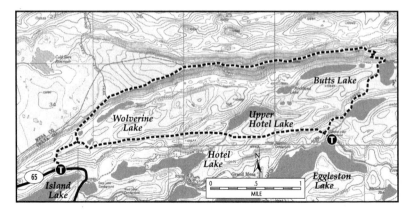

hike only a portion of the trail and forego the topmost crest segment. Your dog must be leashed on the entire loop.

The good news is that a good portion of the trail passes through spruce-pine forest or aspen copses that provide welcome shade on a hot day. There are also several minor stream crossings, enough for your dog to lap water and get his paws wet to stay hydrated.

Hike northeast from the west trailhead through a dense spruce-fir forest to the intersection with the loop in 0.5 mile. Stay left and continue for another 0.6 mile to the intersection with the Cottonwood Lakes Foot Trail. You can turn left here and continue northeast on this trail, foregoing the climb on Crag Crest. This lower trail meanders by several lakes and through lush meadows and aspen groves. It parallels the Crag Crest to the south and offers interesting views of the rocky cockscomb.

For the Crag Crest, continue east, climbing steeply on a narrowing trail as it draws closer to the ridgeline. At the top of the crest the 360-degree vistas are breathtaking over the Grand Mesa and the San Juan and Elk Ranges to the south.

Continue east on the crest until the trail begins to descend. The trail crosses a boulder field. Here extra caution for you and your dog is imperative—watch your footing. These volcanic rocks are leftovers from the ancient lava flow that created the cap forming the top of Grand Mesa, essentially a giant flat-topped mountain.

Next the trail descends in several tight switchbacks that cut across an open hillside with views of the lakes below. From here, complete the loop on nearly level terrain, again through a dense spruce-fir forest. You can exit the loop at the east trailhead at Eggleston Lake, or continue on to the west trailhead.

FOURTEENERS

78. Mount Belford and Mount Oxford

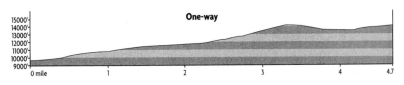

Round trip: 9.4 miles
Hiking time: 9–10 hours
High point: 14,197 feet
Elevation gain: 5000 feet
Best hiking time: July–August
Maps: USGS Mount Harvard and Winfield; Trails Illustrated Buena Vista, Collegiate Peaks (no. 129)
For more information: San Isabel National Forest, Salida Ranger District, (719) 539-3591

Getting there: From Buena Vista, drive north on U.S. Highway 24 for 15 miles. Turn left (west) at Clear Creek Reservoir and proceed 8 miles to Vicksburg at 9700 feet. Small and primitive camp areas are along Clear Creek, east and west of Vicksburg. You may select one to camp overnight or hike up Missouri Gulch to just short of timberline and camp there.

Mount Belford (14,197 feet) is the nineteenth-highest Fourteener and Mount Oxford (14,153 feet) is the twenty-seventh highest. Even with these elevations, both Belford and Oxford have gentle, broad, grass-covered ridges and offer suitable Fourteener beginner climbs for a dog.

Cross Clear Creek on a bridge at Vicksburg and hike south on trail up Missouri Gulch for 2 miles to the head of the gulch. Elkhead Pass will be

One-way

0 mile   1   2   3   4   4.7

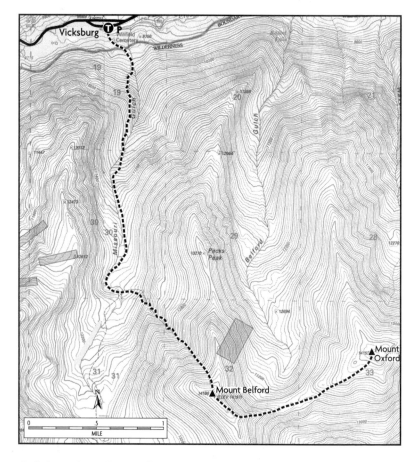

slightly to the right (southwest). Missouri Mountain, another Fourteener, will be on your right (west). The climb up Missouri Gulch is long and tedious. The good part is that once you climb out of the trees, you will find several meadows and the trail will follow a creek.

This is a good time to check the weather, rest, and make sure your dog is cool and has had plenty of water. The hike from here is at high altitude with constant exposure to changing weather and hot temperatures on a sunny day. Sudden, vicious electrical storms are very common and there is no water once you start up the slopes of Mount Belford.

If the sky is clear, continue along the creek trail until you come to a fork. The right (west) fork leads to Elkhead Pass and the left fork (east) is signed "Mount Belford." At 3.3 miles, start ascending the rock wall of Belford. Continue up the improved trail that ascends the rock wall and then crosses the tundra on a steep uphill climb to the reddish rock promontory of the summit.

It is customary to climb Oxford with Belford. From the summit of Belford find the trail that descends into the saddle between Belford and Oxford, and drop a regrettable 350 feet. Continue east-northeast to Oxford on a good climbers' trail. To descend, return to the saddle between Oxford and Belford, reclimb Belford, and descend into Missouri Gulch the way you came.

A glimpse of Oxford from Missouri Gulch

Missouri Mountain might tempt you, but do not do it with your dog. The climb up to the ridge is not hard, but the ridge walk to the summit is narrow and gravelly with sheer drop-off on both sides. A misstep spells trouble for you and your dog. There have been two fatalities on Missouri.

Backpacking: This hike can easily be extended into a multi-night camping adventure. Camp in Missouri Gulch near the creek and just below timberline.

79. Mount Antero

Round trip: 9.2 miles
Hiking time: 8 hours
High point: 14,269 feet
Elevation gain: 3300
Best hiking time: July–August
Maps: USGS Mount Antero and St. Elmo; Trails Illustrated Buena Vista, Collegiate Peaks (no. 129)
For more information: San Isabel National Forest, Salida Ranger District, Phone (719) 539-3591

Getting there: From Buena Vista drive south on U.S. Highway 285 for 8 miles. Turn west on Colorado Highway 162 and drive 9.5 miles to Cascade Campground (good place to camp). Drive another 2.8 miles west on Colorado Highway 162 to Baldwin Gulch Road at 9239 feet near Alpine. Park here if you have a passenger car (and add 5.2 miles to your round trip hike). The Baldwin Gulch Road is on the left (south). It is a rugged old mining road that climbs to 13,000 feet. To avoid hiking up from Alpine, most people use a four-wheel-drive vehicle to drive another 2.6 miles to a fork in the road and a shallow, fordlike crossing of Baldwin Creek. Some passenger vehicles also drive farther on the very rough and narrow road.

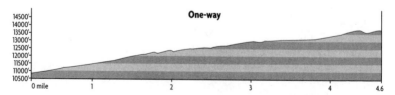

Opposite: On the old mining road when climbing Mount Antero

At 14,269 feet, Mount Antero is the tenth-highest Fourteener. To start, take the left (east) road fork and cross Baldwin Creek. The creek crossing is the last source of reliable water, so make sure your dog is well hydrated and is cool when you start hiking. Continue climbing for 1.3 miles on a steepening terrain before coming to a series of tight, short and steep switchbacks that will tax your stamina and that of your dog for the next 1 mile.

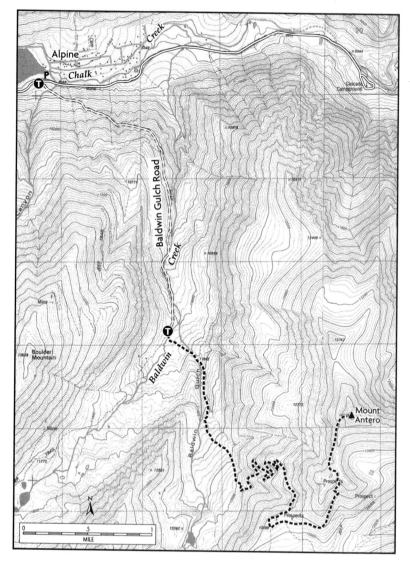

Past the switchbacks, evidence of mining activity is all around you. Quartz, aquamarine, and topaz crystals can be found near the summit of Mount Antero. You may come across geologists and miners prospecting.

Continue climbing Antero's south shoulder to a gem mine. The final 0.5 mile ascent is up a ridge trail through talus. Make sure your dog stays on the trail. Sign the register at the summit and return the way you came.

Backpacking: Extend this hike into an overnight camping adventure by camping near the creek.

80. Handies Peak

Round trip: 7 miles
Hiking time: 6 hours
High point: 14,048 feet
Elevation gain: 3600 feet
Best hiking time: Mid-July–mid-August
Maps: USGS Handies Peak and Redcloud Peak; Trails Illustrated Telluride, Silverton, Ouray, Lake City (no. 141)
For more information: Bureau of Land Management, Gunnison Field Office, (970) 641-0471

Getting there: From Lake City, take Colorado Highway 149 south for 2.5 miles. Turn right onto the road to Lake San Cristobal. Follow the paved road about 4 miles then continue on dirt road for 12.6 miles. The trail sign, located on the left, indicates Handies Peak. The trailhead is at the mouth of Grizzly Creek at 10,400 feet. There is an excellent campsite here with water (not potable) and an outhouse.

Grizzly Gulch Trail is the most popular route to Handies Peak (14,048 feet), one of the five Fourteeners near Lake City. Handies Peak, the fortieth-highest Fourteener, is a big rounded mountain with grassy slopes and wide ridges. In the nineteenth century it was at the heart of silver mining and later was used as pasture by sheep ranchers. Even

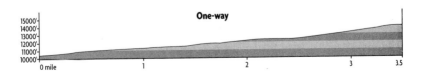

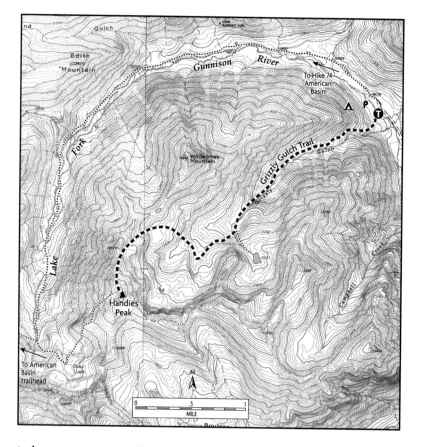

today, you may see a herd of sheep on a distant slope of Whitecross Mountain or on Handies itself.

As with other Fourteeners, once you have climbed above 11,000 or so feet you are above timberline and at the mercy of mountain weather. The only source of water for your dog is along Grizzly Creek, so make sure to take plenty of water along for yourself and your pet.

From the trailhead, cross the Lake Fork of the Gunnison River on a log bridge and strike out southwest on the clearly defined Grizzly Gulch Trail. Climbing steadily, the trail passes through spruce, fir, and aspen forests. At timberline, the trail continues up the basin then climbs the ridge to the west.

The trail forks at 1.75 miles. A small alpine lake is 0.25 mile to the left—good for water if your dog is getting too hot and weary.

On the tundra, rock cairns mark the trail as it climbs upvalley for 0.75

mile. A sign points to a long switchback that turns a hairpin as it ascends to the ridge leading to the summit. Watch for talus along the upper trail around the switchback ridge.

Once on the ridge, turn south to reach the summit and relish the panoramic views of the San Juan Mountains.

Return the way you came or combine this hike with Hike 74 through American Basin for a 10-mile loop. To cut this shorter and to avoid hiking the access road between trailheads, use a car shuttle instead. You can also hike up Handies from American Basin for an easier ascent with only 2700 feet elevation gain.

Backpacking: This hike can easily be extended into a multi-night camping adventure. From the base camp at Grizzly Gulch, explore the vistas, peaks and meadows of the San Juans.

Sheep on a slope near Handies Peak

APPENDIX A:
CONTACT INFORMATION AND RESOURCES

Aspen Center for Environmental
Studies at Hallam Lake
100 Puppy Smith Street
Aspen, CO 81611
(970) 925-5756
aces@aspennature.org

Agencies

Adams County Department of Parks
and Community Resources
977 Henderson Road
Brighton, CO 80610
(303) 637-8000

Arapaho and Roosevelt National
Forests, Pawnee National Grassland
www.fs.fed.us/r2/arnf/

Boulder Ranger District
2140 Yarmouth Avenue
Boulder, CO 80301
(303) 541-2500

Canyon Lakes Ranger District
2150 Centre Avenue, Building E
Fort Collins, CO 80524
(970) 295-6700

Clear Creek Ranger District 101
Chicago Creek Road
P.O. Box 3307
Idaho Springs, CO 80452
(303) 567-3000
www.fs.fed.us/r2/arnf/

Indian Peaks Wilderness
Information Line
(303) 541-2519

Sulfur Ranger District
9 Ten Mile Drive
P.O. Box 10
Granby, CO 80446
(970) 887-4100

Aurora Parks and Open Space
Department
1470 South Havana
Aurora, CO 80012
(303) 739-7160

Boulder County Parks and Open Space
2045 13th Street
Boulder, CO 80202
(303) 441-3950

City of Boulder Open Space &
Mountain Parks Department
P.O. Box 791
Boulder, CO 80306
(303) 441-3440
www.ci.boulder.co.us/openspace/

Bureau of Land Management
Gunnison Field Office
216 North Colorado
Gunnison, CO 81230
(970) 641-0471
www.co.blm.gov

Colorado State Parks
1313 Sherman Street, Room 618
Denver, CO 80203
(303) 866-3437
www.parks.state.co.us

Castlewood Canyon State Park
2989 South State Highway 83
Franktown, CO 80116
(303) 688-5242
castlewood.canyon@state.co.us

Chatfield State Park
11500 North Roxborough Park Road
Littleton, CO 80125
(303) 791-7275 (office phone)
(303) 791-5555 (Chatfield Marina)
(303) 933-3636 (B&B Livery)
chatfld@csn.net

Cherry Creek State Park
4201 South Parker Road
Aurora, CO 80014
(303) 699-3860
chycrk@csn.net

Golden Gate Canyon State Park
3873 Highway 46
Golden, CO 80403
(303) 582-3707
goldgate@csn.net

Denver Water Department (High Line
  Canal owner)
1600 West 12th Avenue
Denver, CO 80204
(303) 628-6170

  Community Relations Office
  (303) 628-6324

  Recreation Office
  (303) 628-6526

Denver Parks and Recreation
  Department (Trails)
2300 15th Street
Denver, CO 80202
(303) 698-4903

Grand Mesa, Uncompahgre, and
  Gunnison National Forests
2250 Highway 50
Delta, CO 81416
(970) 874-6600
www.fs.fed.us/r2/gmug/

  Grand Valley Ranger District
  777 Crossroads Blvd.
  Grand Junction, CO 81506
  (970) 242-8211

  Grand Mesa Visitor Center
  (970) 856-4153

Jefferson County Open Space
700 Jefferson County Parkway
Suite 100
Golden, CO 80401
(303) 271-5925

Pike and San Isabel National Forests
www.fs.fed.us/r2/psicc/sal

  Cimarron National Grassland
  242 East Highway 56
  P.O. Box 300
  (620) 697-4621

  Comanche National Grassland
  Carrizo Unit
  P.O. Box 127
  27204 Highway 287
  Springfield, CO 81073
  (719) 523-6591

  Leadville Ranger District
  2015 North Poplar
  Leadville, CO 80461
  (719) 486-0749

  Pikes Peak Ranger District
  601 South Weber
  Colorado Springs, CO 80903
  (719) 636-1602

  Cimarron and Comanche National
    Grasslands
  Pueblo Supervisors Office
  2840 Kachina Drive
  Pueblo, CO 81008
  (719) 553-1400

  Salida Ranger District
  325 West Rainbow Blvd.
  Salida, CO 81201
  (719) 836-2031
  www.fs.fed.us/r2/sal

  San Carlos Ranger District
  3170 East Main Street
  Canon City, CO 81212
  (719) 836-2031

  South Park Ranger District
  320 Highway 285
  P.O. Box 219
  Fairplay, CO 80440
  (719) 836-2031

South Platte Ranger District
19316 Goddard Ranch Court
Morrison, CO 80465
(303) 697-0414

Routt National Forest
www.fs.fed.us/r2/mbr/

Hahns Peak/Bears Ears Ranger
District
925 Weiss Drive
Steamboat Springs, CO 80487
(970) 879-1870

South Suburban Parks and Recreation
District
6631 South University Blvd.
Centennial, CO 80121
(303) 794-4218

City of Thornton Parks Department
2211 Eppinger Blvd.
Thornton, CO 80229
(303) 538-7632

White River National Forest
www.fs.fed.us/r2/whiteriver/

Aspen Ranger District
806 West Hallam
Aspen, CO 801611
(970) 925-3445

Dillon Ranger District
680 Blue River Parkway
P.O. Box 620
Silverthorne, CO 80498
(970) 468-5400

Holy Cross Ranger District
24747 U.S. Highway 24
Minturn, CO 81645
(970) 827-5715

Private Organizations

Colorado Fourteeners Initiative
710 10th Street, Suite 220
Golden, CO 80401
(303) 278-7525
www.coloradofourteeners.org

Colorado Mountain Club
710 10th Street, Suite 200
Golden, CO 80401
(303) 279-3080
(800) 633-4417
www.cmc.org

South Platte River Greenway
Foundation
1666 South University Blvd., Suite B
Denver, CO 80210
(303) 698-1322

Leave No Trace Center for Outdoor
Ethics
P.O. Box 997
Boulder, CO 80306
(800) 332-4100
www.lnt.org

Pets R Permitted

Hotel and Motel Directory
P.O. Box 3930
Torrence CA 90510-3930
(310) 374-6246
MENelson@Flash.Net,
PetExpert@RocketMail.Com

BIBLIOGRAPHY

Borneman, Walter R. and Lyndon J. Lampert. *Climbing Guide to Colorado's Fourteeners*. Boulder, Colorado: Pruett Publishing Company, 1984.

Garratt, Mike and Bob Martin. *Colorado's High Thirteeners*. Evergreen, Colorado: Cordillera Press, Inc., 1984.

Jacob, Randy. *The Colorado Trail, The Official Guidebook*. Englewood, Colorado: Westcliffe Publishers, 1994.

Johnson, Richard H., ed. *The Guide to the High Line Canal*. Denver, Colorado: Denver Water Community Relations Office, 1999.

Koch, Don. *The Colorado Pass Book*, 3rd ed., Boulder, Colorado: Pruett Publishing Company, 2000.

Noel, Thomas J., Paul F. Mahoney and Richard E. Stevens. *Historical Atlas of Colorado*. Norman, Oklahoma: University of Oklahoma Press, 1994.

Ormes, Robert M. and Randy Jacobs. *Guide to the Colorado Mountains*. Golden, Colorado: Colorado Mountain Club, 2000.

Roach, Gerry. *Colorado's Fourteeners: From Hikes to Climbs,* 2nd ed., Golden, Colorado: Fulcrum Publishing, 1999.

Roach, Gerry, and Jennifer Burns. *Colorado's Thirteeners: 13,800 to 13,999 Feet, from Hikes to Climbs*. Golden. Colorado: Fulcrum Publishing, 2001.

Savage, Ania, ed. *Colorado Mountain Club Pocket Guide to the Colorado 14ers*, upd. ed., Boulder, Colorado: Johnson Books, 1997.

Wolf, James R. *Guide to the Continental Divide Trail*. Baltimore, Maryland: Continental Divide Trail Society, 1997.

INDEX

ABOUT THE AUTHOR

Ania Savage is a journalist by training and a hiker by avocation. She moved to Colorado in the 1980s and soon joined the Colorado Mountain Club, where she is still a member and frequent participant in "doggie hikes." Over the years, she has climbed thirty of Colorado's fifty-four Fourteeners and more than fifty other Colorado mountains. She has hiked in Patagonia and on the Appalachian Trail, where she climbed her first mountain, Mount Marcy, as a teenager.

Ania is the author of two previous hiking guides for Colorado and her travel memoir, *Return to Ukraine,* was a finalist for the Colorado Book Award in 2001. She teaches at the University of Denver.

(Photo by Yue Savage)

THE MOUNTAINEERS, founded in 1906, is a nonprofit outdoor activity and conservation club, whose mission is "to explore, study, preserve, and enjoy the natural beauty of the outdoors. . . ." Based in Seattle, Washington, the club is now the third-largest such organization in the United States, with seven branches throughout Washington State.

The Mountaineers sponsors both classes and year-round outdoor activities in the Pacific Northwest, which include hiking, mountain climbing, ski-touring, snowshoeing, bicycling, camping, kayaking, nature study, sailing, and adventure travel. The club's conservation division supports environmental causes through educational activities, sponsoring legislation, and presenting informational programs.

All club activities are led by skilled, experienced instructors, who are dedicated to promoting safe and responsible enjoyment and preservation of the outdoors.

If you would like to participate in these organized outdoor activities or the club's programs, consider a membership in The Mountaineers. For information and an application, write or call The Mountaineers, Club Headquarters, 300 Third Avenue West, Seattle, WA 98119; (206) 284-6310. You can also visit the club's website at *www.mountaineers.org* or contact The Mountaineers via email at *clubmail@mountaineers.org*.

The Mountaineers Books, an active, nonprofit publishing program of the club, produces guidebooks, instructional texts, historical works, natural history guides, and works on environmental conservation. All books produced by The Mountaineers Books fulfill the club's mission.

Send or call for our catalog of more than 500 outdoor titles:

The Mountaineers Books
1001 SW Klickitat Way, Suite 201
Seattle, WA 98134
800-553-4453
mbooks@mountaineersbooks.org
www.mountaineersbooks.org

OTHER TITLES YOU MIGHT ENJOY FROM
THE MOUNTAINEERS BOOKS

Best Hikes with Children: Colorado, *Maureen Keilty*
Short hikes for short legs (and those still young at heart) in Colorado.

100 Classic Hikes in Colorado,
Scott S. Warren
A full color guide to the best hikes in the state.

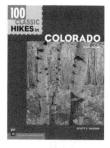

Hiking Colorado's Geology,
Ralph & Lindy Hopkins
Explore the unique and spectacular geologic formations of Colorado.

Don't Forget the Duct Tape: Tips and Tricks for Repairing Outdoor Gear,
Kristin Hostetter
Pack this little guide with you and be an instant outdoor fixit guru!

**Digital Photography Outdoors:
A Field Guide for Travel & Adventure Photographers,** *James Martin*
Special techniques for outdoor adventure shooting—making the most of digital's advantages

Also in the Best Hikes with Dogs Series:

Bay Area and Beyond,
Thom Gabrukiewicz
Inland Northwest,
*Craig Romano &
Alan L. Bauer*
Western Washington,
Dan A. Nelson
Oregon, *Ellen Morris Bishop*
Arizona, *Renée Guillory*